CHASING DREAMS

Living My Life
One Yard At a Time

Jerry Kill
with Jim Bruton

TRIUMPH
B O O K S

Library of Congress Cataloging-in-Publication Data

Names: Kill, Jerry, 1961– author. | Bruton, James H., 1945– co-author.
Title: Chasing dreams : living my life one yard at a time / Jerry Kill, with Jim Bruton.
Description: Chicago, Illinois : Triumph Books LLC, [2016] | Includes bibliographical references and index.
Identifiers: LCCN 2016030421 | ISBN 9781629372754 (alk. paper)
Subjects: LCSH: Kill, Jerry, 1961– | Football coaches—United States—Biography. | Athletic directors—United States--Biography.
Classification: LCC GV939.K42 A3 2016 | DDC 796.332092 [B]—dc23
LC record available at https://lccn.loc.gov/2016030421

This book is available in quantity at special discounts for your group or organization. For further information, contact:
Triumph Books LLC
814 North Franklin Street
Chicago, Illinois 60610
(312) 337–0747
www.triumphbooks.com

Printed in U.S.A.
ISBN: 978-1-62937-275-4

Photo credits: first insert, page 4 (top) courtesy of *Webb City Sentinel*; insert page 4 (bottom) courtesy of Pittsburg State University; page 5 (top) courtesy of Saginaw Valley State University; page 5 (bottom) courtesy of Emporia State University; page 6 (top and bottom) courtesy of Southern Illinois University; page 7 (top and bottom) courtesy of Woody Thorne, Southern Illinois Healthcare; page 8, courtesy of Northern Illinois University.

Second insert, pages 1–3, 6 courtesy of the University of Minnesota; page 4 (top and bottom), 5 (top and bottom) courtesy of the Epilepsy Foundation of Minnesota; page 5 (center) courtesy of Deb Hadley.

All other photos are courtesy of the author.

With great love and appreciation I dedicate this book to my wonderful family, truly the loves of my life. To my wife, Rebecca, and my daughters, Krystal and Tasha, you have made my life more special than you will ever know.

And to my very exceptional mom and dad, and my brother, Frank, and sister-in-law, Cindy, I thank you and am deeply appreciative for all the caring and love you have given me during my life. I will be forever grateful.

I further dedicate this book to all the coaches, teams, players, staff, media, and friends who have entered my life over the years and have made a difference to me in such a positive way. Without you, nothing I did would have had any importance or made a difference.

And last but not least, I am so appreciative of the influence of you, the Man Upstairs, and how you have affected my life and my faith in such creative and powerful ways. Your influence, guidance, and love are daily occurrences, and I thank you.

"Sometimes the games just get in the way. Developing these young men is much more important."

Contents

Foreword

NOTHING IS MORE CRITICAL TO an athletic department than the leadership of its head coaches.

Very directly, coaches influence the overall spirit of the department; play a vital role in maintaining a positive, ethical culture; and, most important, shape the experiences and the lives of each student-athlete. The right cultural fit is imperative.

During 2007 at Northern Illinois University, following an exhaustive search, we hired a tremendously accomplished football coach from FCS Southern Illinois University. Jerry Kill is an outstanding football coach who has won at every stop on his football journey and, more critically, in life. At Northern Illinois University he turned the Huskies into a 10-win team less than three years into his tenure. But as influential as he has been on the football field, it was Coach Kill's off-the-field characteristics that assured me he was a phenomenal choice to lead the program.

Coach Kill is precisely the type of person you would choose to have mentor your son or daughter. He is genuine, sincere, honest, values-driven, humble, and passionate. His perseverance, dedication, ethics, and morality are unmatched. He is the ultimate family man, and a father figure to many. He has made a remarkable impact on hundreds of young men during his career, and there is no doubt about the effect he will continue to have on people each day of his life.

A person's life is forever changed for the better when Jerry Kill and his wife, Rebecca, come into it. To be certain, I am fortunate to have called Jerry a colleague and am blessed to continue to call him a friend.

—Jim Phillips
Vice President for Athletics & Recreation
Northwestern University

Foreword

IT HAS BEEN STATED MANY times that the true testament of the greatness of a man, a friend, or a coach is that when he is around, everyone is better because of his presence. My friend Jerry Kill is that man, that friend, and that coach! I personally thank him for being there for me and for so many others.

The definition of what a college football coach represents is multifaceted, and not much different from what it means to be a husband or father. To be brutally honest, it is a hard task to be great at all three, but Jerry has always had the ability to do just that and excel.

Coaches spend so much time helping raise other families' sons and daughters and winning games that we sometimes forget what drove us to this game, which was our first love: *people!* Jerry has never forgotten the people who helped him along the way, and his love, appreciation, and gratitude to them is forever lasting.

I sit here today a better man, husband, dad, and coach because of my friendship with Jerry Kill. I hope as you read his book you will come to know the Jerry Kill and the Kill family as I have.

Jerry defied many odds to be who he has become today.

—Gary Patterson
Head Coach, Texas Christian University

Foreword

JERRY KILL IS A TURNAROUND artist. He's a fixer, a builder, a renovator, and a repairman. He takes broken football programs and makes them well. Very well. And as much as his life has been defined by his football coaching exploits, he's an even better man, a better person, than his on-field exploits reveal. When I hired him to fix our broken football program at Southern Illinois University in 2000, I knew I was getting a good football coach. But I didn't quite realize the breadth and depth of the rest of the package. I witnessed the devotion of his student-athletes, the loyalty of his core staff, and the appreciation of his fans, as well as Jerry's dedication to all those people, as well as to his family, his faith, and the "great game of college football," as Jerry is wont to say.

In the pages that follow, you will read about Jerry's accomplishments, about his challenges, and about his experiences and how they have shaped him. More important, you will be touched by his spirit, his compassion, and his integrity and, along the way, be entertained, moved, and inspired. You'll understand why so many of us have so much respect and admiration for him. This is a remarkable story about a remarkable man.

—Paul Kowalczyk
Former Director of Athletics, Southern Illinois University

Coauthor's Note

THIS IS THE AUTOBIOGRAPHY OF Jerry Kill *in his own words.* Some of the sentence structure and grammar may be technically out of sorts to some extent, but as Coach Kill has said, "I always get accused of rewriting the English language."

Acknowledgments

I WANT TO SAY TO all the people who have been so good to me throughout the years, you have helped me more than I ever helped you. You mean so much to me and my family, and I wish I could thank each of you by name, but there are too many to mention.

I want to thank everybody who has ever worked with me, on and off the field. You have been a blessing. My deepest thanks goes to the administrations, college and high school coaches throughout the country, trainers, equipment people, those who kept the building clean, support staff, the media, fans, donors, students, colleagues, my entire family, and my friends.

To Sid Hartman, when you are 96 years old and still "walking the beat," so to speak, you must be something special. And that you are, Sid! In my 32 years of coaching, I have never worked with a finer media representative or had a better relationship. I feel sincerely blessed for the five years you have been in Rebecca's and my life, and I deeply thank you with all my heart. You're the best, Sid, and you will always be my close, personal friend!

Most important, I want to thank the players, because without the players, you have no game. I thank you personally—every one of you who ever stepped on the field and put the shoulder pads and helmet on for Coach Kill. I thank you if you played a lot or didn't, if you were an All-American or just a part of the team, whether you were someone where football wasn't in your heart and you moved on. You have all been a part of my life. You made me better, and I love you from the bottom of my heart. For 32 years you made me want to get up in the morning and go to work, because it never was work. Football became my passion because of you. Thanks for the great memories. I want you to know when I walked off the field for the last time, you all walked off with me.

The writing of this book was a labor of love. First, thanks go to my coauthor, Jim Bruton, for the time and effort and travel he has put into the book and for all the extra work involved. There would not be a book without his commitment and if we had not worked so well together during the process.

I also want to thank Triumph Books and their dedicated staff for all their expertise and for having the confidence in my story to take on this project.

And a sincere thank-you to all those who contributed to the book, both for their contribution and for the tremendous influence that each of these people has had on my life. I cannot express my love and appreciation enough or communicate what each of these people has personally meant to me.

And last, to utilize the term "acknowledgment" is an understatement to what my family has meant to me, been to me, and will continue to be for the rest of my life. Words will never be able to express my deepest thoughts and feelings about my closest loved ones. I am thankful to each one and for my faith and to God for creating us, guiding us, and keeping us together for all these years.

—Jerry Kill

OVER THE COURSE OF WORKING with Jerry Kill on this book, I had the opportunity to talk with countless numbers of people who have crossed paths with Coach Kill. I only wish there was enough paper and time to record everything I was told; there is not. The following paragraphs are derived from comments, superlatives, and testimonials from those interviewed for this book.

"It's hard to know where to begin" was a dominant theme throughout the interviews. Over and over again, I heard comments such as, "He makes you feel special," "If you charted his relationships, they would be off the charts," and "He is trustworthy, loyal, honest, credible, unique, and the fairest person I know." Words and phrases used to describe Coach Kill's character in my interviews included "integrity," "greatness," "the best," "caring," "competitive," "genuine," "respect," "inspiring," "motivating," "sincere," "someone who listens," and "one of a kind."

I also heard: "Spend two hours with him and you will think he is your best friend," "He has a huge heart," "He would do anything for anybody," "He is the finest human being I have ever known," and, "If I was in a fox hole with my life on the line, I would want Jerry Kill next to me."

Personal accounts from colleagues and friends included: "He shaped me as a man," "I would lay down my life for him," "He takes care of his staff like family," "I would run through a wall for him," "I owe all my success in my life to Coach Kill," "He taught me about education, kindness, and how to set a good example," and "He's a great coach but a better person, and I always want to be around him."

If all of us could act in a fashion that emulates even a small portion of the predominating thoughts and messages about Jerry Kill, the world would be a better place and Coach Kill would be thrilled. He has set the bar high, lived up to his beliefs, and affected others more than he will ever know.

A special thank-you to each of the following for sharing their memories of Coach Kill: George Adzick, Brian Anderson, Jordan Bazant, Tim Beck, Briean Boddy-Calhoun, Chuck Broyles, Jim Carter, Joe Christensen, Jon Christenson, Tracy Claeys, Adam Clark, David Cobb, Jake Coffman, Connor Cosgrove, Mark Dantonio, Gerry DiNardo, Wayne Drash, Dennis Franchione, Phil Gattone, Mia Gerold, Meredith Gretch, Marquis Grey, Milessa

Haab, Nick Hill, Maddie Hayes, Chandler Harnish, Sid Hartman, Rich Jantz, Jeff Jones, Eric Klein, Vicki Kopplin, Paul Kowalczyk, Ron Lankford, Mitch Leidner, Matt Limegrover, Roger Lipe, Sharon Lipe, Joel Maturi, Carl Mauck, Mike Max, KJ Maye, Billy Miller, Maja Nord, Dan O'Brien, Casey O'Brien, Trevor Olson, Jeff Phelps, Pat Poore, Kammy Powell, Angie Reeves, Rob Reeves, Mike Reis, Steve Richardson, John Roderique, Dickie Rolls, Mark Rosen, Joel Sambursky, T. Denny Sanford, Jay Sawvel, Bart Scott, Bob Stein, Mike Sherels, Dr. Brien Smith, Doug Smith, Mark Smith, Paul Spicer, Kurt Thompson, Woody Thorne, Rick Utter, Tom Waske, Kent Weiser, Pete Westerhaus, Maxx Williams, Gerald Young, and Jim Zebrowki. Thank you also to all of you who provided photos.

In starting this project, I believed I was coauthoring an autobiography of a very successful football coach who has turned around multiple programs and who had to battle both cancer and epilepsy along the way. And this is all true, no question about that. However, what I found through my interviews with Coach Jerry Kill's colleagues, acquaintances, former players, coaches, and numerous others who have come in contact with him is that the real story is the incredibly positive and forever-lasting impact he has had on others.

I have followed and played sports my whole life; I am a huge lifelong fan. And even though professional football, baseball, basketball, and hockey franchises have collectively dominated my interests, I proudly confess that Minnesota Golden Gophers football has always been number one on my list.

I attended my first Gophers football game in 1955 and later was fortunate enough to play in a couple games in the mid 1960s and become a member of the M Club. Having said that, to have had the opportunity to work with former Gophers football coach Jerry Kill on his book has been an honor and thrill beyond words.

—Jim Bruton

| one |

The Family Roots

IF I HAD IT TO do over, I wouldn't change a thing. I've been very fortunate in my life, and when I look back, I believe that everything that has happened to me has happened for a reason, including where I came from.

I was born in 1961 in Wichita, Kansas, and I have a brother, Frank, who is four years younger than me. We lived just outside Wichita on Westfield in a very small house in a great neighborhood. My dad, Jim Kill, was never really happy with the area because he wanted to move out to the country.

Our first move to a little more country living during the early years of my life was to Goddard, Kansas. It had a population of a little more than 4,000 people, and we lived there until I was in the seventh grade, at which point we moved to Cheney, Kansas.

But I honestly believe the basic roots of my life can be traced to before I was even born, to my dad and all the way back to Elk Falls, Kansas, the community of less than 100 people where he was from. We went there to visit often, and it was in Elk Falls that my dad's family had a great influence on me and who I am today.

We lived fairly close to both my grandparents, the Kills and the McGinnises. We loved fishing with Grandpa Kill and going to his house over in Elk Falls. And when we visited, my grandma would cook up these great meals. And let me tell you, she could cook, and those Kill boys could eat. And another thing: you better believe those Kill boys were going to be in church on Sunday. That was the deal. We went to the Catholic church every Sunday and then got the fishing poles out and headed for Wildcat Creek. The creek was full of catfish and lots of bullheads, and we would spend hours there.

We would also go into town and sit around at the local gas station by ourselves, or sometimes with one of my dad's friends. The highlight of going into Elk Falls was buying Bit-O-Honey bars. I think they are still sold in some places. And they had a pop machine with Chocolate Soldier pop. I bet I could ask a hundred people today and no one would have heard of Chocolate Soldier. Back in the day, that was our drink of choice.

I think the last recorded population of Elk Falls was 99 people, so you can see it wasn't very big. But I cannot think of a time when we didn't have things to do. I always looked forward to our out-of-town trips and going to see my grandparents there.

My dad didn't have an education, but he was very smart. He had three brothers—Bob, Jack, and Don—and they were all tough; they didn't lose any fights in their day. They were hardworking and a real reflection of their parents, my Grandma and Grandpa Kill, who were hard-nosed, give-it-all-you-got farmers.

When he wasn't working on the farm, my grandpa worked part-time and drove a yellow bus well into his sixties, and my grandma managed the house, canned food, and generally took care of the family. I mean these were hardworking, strong, tough people. Grandma was a phenomenal cook, and when we went down there to visit, we ate. She made us a lot of fried food, and we ate her canned food; we really had some good home-cooked meals. My grandma lived into her upper nineties, and I think she could have whipped all our asses if she had wanted to. She ruled the ship, no doubt about it.

Grandma and Grandpa Kill had a huge influence on my dad becoming the kind of person he was, and it carried over to me. I learned from my dad and his family. As I said, these were hard-nosed people who weren't afraid to work. And my dad and his brothers were the same way.

My dad and his brothers learned the basics of their life from Grandma and Grandpa Kill. None of them ever had a formal education. Instead they got an education on living every single day, and none of it was easy. Hard work, a great attitude, and taking care of family—that was their education.

As a kid, I admired everything about my dad and his brothers, who all got along well. I watched them, and I wanted to emulate their toughness and lifestyle. I got to be around them a great deal because we spent a lot of time visiting each other's families.

Their life was not easy. It was farming, cattle ranching, and tough living. They were salt-of-the-earth people, and my dad and his brothers were all strong and physical. I got the opportunity to watch my dad and my Uncles Bob and Jack get up early in the morning and work. They would work the cattle, feed the cattle, and do all the other things farm folks do…and it didn't matter what the weather was. I mean they would work and work hard if it was 10 degrees or 110 degrees outdoors. It didn't matter to them. It was what they did. They were going to work from dawn until night. And when they got home, Grandma would have food on the table. My dad's other brother, Uncle Don, worked for Boeing, and he never cheated the workday either.

There was an interesting thing about Dad and his brothers. They were kind of like cowboys. I mean we seemed to *always* be at a rodeo, and I think Dad always wished he was a full-time cowboy and likely wanted his boys to follow suit. There was something about that tough, competitive lifestyle that intrigued Dad.

I was very close to my dad. But I will say that he was a guy that could scare the hell out of you just by looking at you. He was intense and if he heard one of his boys didn't do a good job baling hay or whatever it was, he could really get fired up. He didn't believe in that. He didn't have any tolerance for anything but perfection. He was so tough that I recall once he broke a bone in his foot and didn't even go to the doctor. He wasn't going to let that stop him. I mean he broke a bone in his damn foot and he just put his shoe on and went to work.

Dad was a tough guy, but he had a softer side too. He was the type of guy who planted this huge garden on our property, worked that garden hard, and then gave most of it away. He would help anybody out.

For us a big treat was going with the family to Wichita, especially for ice cream. We really looked forward to those trips to the Dairy Queen or to the A&W. That was our big outing, and it always seemed like those root beer floats or ice cream cones never lasted long enough.

We would ride there in the back of Dad's old pickup truck. And I mean it was an old truck. Dad never, and I mean never, bought anything close to a new truck. It was a total wreck, but it got us to where we were going. The frame was all bent up and there was rust and dents. I always wondered why we didn't spend half our life stranded somewhere.

I had such admiration for my entire family and received some great mentoring. We often had family reunions, and I mean big ones. We either had them at Uncle Jack's place or in Moline, Kansas, at the Catholic church, and all the Kills would come. They were great reunions, and everyone had wonderful connections with each other.

It was the closeness of our family and their work ethic that stood out for me. It was how my dad and uncles had been raised. My brother, Frank, and I both saw all this as kids, and it rubbed off on us. Close family, toughness, and loyalty. They had it all, and it affected us.

Dad would chew your ass out for whatever you did, and then mom would be there to clean things up. Things back then weren't like they are today. If we stepped out of line, dad might take a belt to your ass. You were simply going to do what you were supposed to do. If you got in trouble at school, it was worse. After dad finished with us, mom would come by and tell us it was going to be all right. She kind of babied us to be sure we were going to make it through.

When we went over to my mom's side of the family in Goddard, Kansas, where she was raised, we saw some different aspects of living. And they had a great impact also. My mom's name was Sonja, but sometimes people called her Sandy, and I knew she never liked that. She always preferred to be called Sonja. Mom did it all. She was a great mom, as I said—a great cook and was there to see that everything was going to work out. She used to babysit for money and sometimes would take care of five or six kids at a time.

Mom didn't have a college education, and neither did Grandma and Grandpa McGinnis. My grandpa was a construction worker and my grandma was a librarian at the high school. She kept the books at home and was good at keeping everyone in line. And again, like the Kills, these were people who knew how to work.

My Grandpa McGinnis looked kind of Spanish American, never wore a shirt in the summer, and was called Pancho by everybody. And let me tell you, he could make a living. He would be up on top of buildings or houses when it was 100 degrees or more putting in long days. And again, I watched all this and really understood. I saw it from both sides of the family, and it made an impression.

Grandpa McGinnis knew how to build things, and he always did it with the cheapest possible lumber. He would go over to Starr Lumber and grab stuff that others had thrown away, but let me tell you, he knew what he was doing and he built great houses.

My mom is a product of her own family, the McGinnises, who were all very close and very caring people. They had to earn everything they had. Her brother Cal—a very intelligent, well-educated schoolteacher—passed away a few years ago from a seizure, and her other brother, my Uncle Al, was a construction guy like my grandpa. Her sisters were Barbara and Roxanne, all hard workers and good people.

As with the Kill side of the family, the McGinnis family was also very close. We got together with the McGinnises especially around the holidays, and we often went out to Colorado with them and stayed at a place between the Spanish Peaks, composed of the West Spanish Peak and the East Spanish Peak. We would fish the streams, climb mountains, and get the most out of the outdoors. My half-brother, Jimmy, from a previous marriage of my dad's, would go with us to Colorado on occasion.

My mom is a good, thoughtful person and has always been the caregiver of the family; I'm sure she learned it from her mom. Mom took care of people and still does to this day. I mean if someone is sick, Mom is there for them. This was true for me when I had cancer and at other times. She was at my dad's side when he was sick with cancer too, and she never left him until the day he died.

I got a lot of that from Mom and from Grandma and Grandpa McGinnis. I mean Grandpa would give anybody the shirt off his back. (I'm just thinking here—maybe that's why he never wore a shirt.) Seriously, though, he was a kindhearted guy who would help anybody out that needed it. He had good friends and great respect, and he loved people. He would always get in trouble with Grandma, though, because he chewed Beech-Nut tobacco. He would chew inside, and Grandma would get mad and chase him outside.

I worked for my Grandpa McGinnis building houses, and it was one of the greatest experiences I ever had, learning things and being around him. I stayed with Grandma and Grandpa McGinnis for a while and worked for almost a year back around the seventh grade, and I learned a lot. It was another great experience for me.

My mom and dad met while Dad was working for my Grandpa McGinnis. Dad and Grandpa McGinnis always got along great, so it was a good fit. I mean my grandpa knew how hard my dad could work, so he knew my mom was going to be in good hands.

Coming from the Kills and the McGinnises, I had great roots. I learned how to work and I learned about the toughness that came with it, both physically and mentally. That's where it all started. It was my making, and as I look back I could not be more pleased and proud. I am who I am because of my mom and my dad. I wouldn't change a single thing about them. I couldn't ask for more than that.

I had a great childhood. We would do just about everything a kid could do. The neighborhood games—football, basketball, baseball—would always be at our house. As kids, we *played*. What I mean is we were out doing stuff all the time. If we weren't working, we were playing, and playing hard.

I don't think we see the same thing today with kids. All the cell phones, social media, and all that has changed the way kids grow up today, and I think they miss something. It's a shame, because kids today miss something important in life.

Both my parents liked sports, and they really supported everything I did in that regard. Actually, sports was the only thing I did that dad allowed me to do that kept me out of work. He let me off for sports. He liked that. We played basketball, baseball, and football, and he was always there watching. And he was a great athlete in his own right. I recall him playing on his work basketball team, and he could flat-out shoot the ball.

Dad was always there to fire up the competitive spirit in us and keep sports on our plates. We would play ball with just the three of us. Dad would pitch, I would hit, and Frank would chase, and then we would all switch. I can remember we had a basketball hoop and dad wouldn't let us come in the house until we made so many free throws in a row.

I loved all sports and really followed the college teams. Kansas State and Kansas didn't win a lot of games, so I was never a Kansas fan. Because we were not very far from the Oklahoma border, I was really into Oklahoma Sooners football. They were our team.

Barry Switzer was the coach then, and he won a lot of football games. This was after the Bud Wilkinson years and all those great teams, consecutive winning streaks, and all that. They won 40-some games in a row with Bud Wilkinson. He is legendary in Oklahoma.

I never got to any games, but they were on TV, so I got to see all their games that way. We didn't have the means to go to games, but my brother and I would play in the backyard and he would be one player and I would be another. We loved those Sooners.

I was a Kansas City Royals fan too, and a big-time St. Louis Cardinals fan. I could give you the whole Cardinals and Royals rosters. I followed it that closely. Grandpa Kill was real country folk, and he used to lay out in the yard on an old gunnysack swing and listen to the Royals games. I can still see him laying out there pulling for Kansas City.

Most of the time we would play football at home, and it got pretty rough. The games were usually five-on-five, and it often got bloody. We had no padding of any kind, and we would just go at it. I was about 10 years old at the time, and my brother, Frank, who was only 6, would be on the same team as me, and we went to war with our opponents. Even way back then, I wanted to win. As far back as I can remember, losing was never acceptable. And you know what? I think we were pretty much undefeated in the neighborhood.

I can recall getting into fights during games, and sometimes for other reasons. There was this neighborhood kid who always found a way to get everybody mad, so I would fight him. He would run home and tell his mom, and she would tell my mom, who would get all concerned about it. As for Dad, it never bothered him.

Mom would be saying to Dad, "Well, you know, the boys got in some trouble today playing football. I mean they got in some fights, and I think they need to go down and apologize." And Dad would just say, "No, they don't need to go apologize to anyone. That's all part of being a kid." That was the difference between my folks: Mom always wanted us to be good kids and all that, and Dad wanted us to be good kids but to be tough and not take anything from anybody. That was his way.

When we weren't busy working, playing sports, or fishing, we spent time riding Dad's horse, Pete. I think Dad wanted us to be rodeo guys, and he would put us on the horse and old Pete would buck us right off. We never did stay on that horse. Dad was convinced his kids were going to be bareback riders and bull riders and who knows what else. "Get back on," he would tell us, and off we would go. On and off, on and off. That was one area in which we never lived up to Dad's expectations. I guess it's why my brother, Frank, wants nothing to do with horses. Dad tried to stick us on everything he could, but we didn't ride very well. He even had a Brahma bull that was meaner than hell, and I truly believe he thought about putting us on him too, but he never did.

Dad made every possible effort to make us men while Mom was there teaching us the manners side of life the best she could. She taught us how to "be proper in the general public," so to speak, while we got all the hard-nosed toughness from Dad.

Our home in Goddard had gotten us a little more country living, but Dad was not content. He wanted to be even more out in the country, so we moved to Cheney, a town 15 miles away with a population of about 2,000 in the 1970s. And Dad was happy, because we were out in the country.

Dad was all country. He loved country music, and we got into it with him. I recall listening to Ray Price, Hank Williams, and Charley Pride, and I still enjoy them to this day. And we learned about dancing from Mom and Dad. I mean, let me tell you, my mom and dad could flat-out cut a rug! They could dance! They used to go to the Cotillion Ballroom in Wichita, and sometimes they would take us with them. And Rebecca and I still like to dance some and have a great time with it. I've even been known to do a little dancing after a big football win!

It all fit well for dad. Dad was looking for a country town in which to raise his family, and he found it. He wanted a place to keep "his boys" out of trouble and have a country experience. My grandpa and my dad built our house, and back then I suppose it was worth maybe $20,000. As I said, my grandpa was in the building business, so it worked out well for us.

As Dad was building the house, we lived in a little apartment right across from the school. It was a little duplex, and we were all on top of each other. None of it mattered to me. I was a happy kid and enjoyed every part of my life. I had great friends, a great mom and dad, and a great brother, and I had a lot of fun.

We had a great home. My dad had purchased about three acres. Our house sat on a hill with a creek that ran nearby. Behind the house were railroad tracks. We had enough land to have cattle, and there were always a few pigs; I loved it. Those cattle were like Dad's babies. And we had cats out in the barn and a couple rat terriers that he called his "snake dogs." Dad was in his element.

When I look back on Wichita or my years in Goddard, I don't call either of those cities home. My home is Cheney, Kansas. My mom still lives in Cheney, my brother lives in Cheney, and when I visit, I know I'm home.

I liked living in Cheney because I felt like I was with the real people of the world, the working class. These are the farmers and the construction workers. There is so much community passion in Cheney, and that's what Dad wanted; he wanted his boys to belong to a community and to learn to work hard, like he did.

Dad worked two jobs. He would be up at 5:00 every morning and worked until sundown. He worked at Cessna Aircraft on the flight line for 39 years in Wichita, which was about 30 minutes away. I don't know all the details of exactly what he did, but I know it had to do with the aircraft parts.

The Cessna company has been headquartered in Wichita since way back in the late 1920s. They are known for building small planes, and they also build business jets. In the summertime, when Dad took some vacation, he spent it cutting wheat. He worked at his friend Fred Foley's place. And to this very day they still talk about my dad and say he was the best worker they ever had, and I know the people over there at Cessna felt the same way about him.

Fred Foley can tell stories about Jim Kill all day, and I mean all day. He always likes to tell about the time that a bad storm went through the area. It was bad enough so people went to their storm shelters. After it was over, Dad apparently went around to everyone's house in the area to be sure they were all okay. When he got to Fred's place he told Fred, "You better take a look at your house when you get a chance because the whole east side of it's gone." Fred ran outside and found a corner of the roof was torn up some. Dad had told him the whole east side of his house was missing! I guess Dad just thought the damage was pretty severe.

Another time, I really cut up my lip; it was a mess. Dad was going to take care of it right away. He told me, "Go get in the car. We're going to see a friend of mine who is a doctor. He'll fix you up." The doctor he knew was a veterinarian. I said, "The guy is a vet. He's not sewing up my lip!" Mom stepped in and saved me.

Here is another of my favorites: One day my brother, Frank, and I were in the house and Dad came up to us and said, "Gonna paint the house." So we went out and got all the stuff together, and Frank and I started painting. And it wasn't long before I missed a spot. Dad saw it and threw a fit. "Gimme those brushes and I'll show you how to paint!" he groused. He painted the whole damn house while Frank and I watched. And then later when we went into town, he told all his buddies, "The boys and I painted the whole house today!" He was proud as could be. Hell, we barely got our brushes wet.

Dad was the type that no matter what we did he wanted us to do it better. He really drove us to be tough and do things the right way. I mean we busted our asses in just about everything we did.

Dad taught us that. One day he said to us, "You know those Foley boys, now they are something. They bust their asses every single day." I didn't like to hear that and blurted out, "Well, why don't you go and adopt them then!"

Of course, we were all very tight with the Foleys. Dad always drove the old combines for Fred Foley, the ones with the open face. He got us introduced to the farming business and we got into it by baling hay. I think the going rate was two cents a bale or something like that. It was how we made summer money back then. We also pulled rye, and Fred Foley had sheep at his place, so we would go out and catch the sheep for shearing. It kept us busy as kids, and it wasn't easy. Dad had things figured out. He knew what he was doing, and he had a plan for his boys.

We did our chores up in the barn when it was more than 100 degrees outside. We did a lot of things around the farming community too, like baling hay, pulling rye, those kinds of things. My brother also worked at a grain elevator, a really tough job. We were always doing something, and work became a part of our life. We worked many days all day and were treated like men. We even had a beer from time to time. I guess Dad figured if we were 16 and old enough to work, we could drink a beer as well.

Our next-door neighbors in Cheney were the Gordons. Don Gordon—we always called him Big D—worked at Cessna Aircraft with Dad. Don and his wife, Nete, lived in the city of Wichita, and Nete was more of a city girl. But Don and Dad were all country, and they became great friends. Our whole families became great friends. And because of that, both our families had bought land simultaneously and moved together to the big metropolis of Cheney, Kansas.

At our new home in Cheney, we had a fireplace, and dad and Don were always doing something like cutting wood and working together. And then our other neighbors would come over and we would all cut wood, hang out, and just have a good old time.

Back in Goddard, like Cheney, we lived in a really neat neighborhood with a lot of good kids, and when it came to baseball season, most of us were big St. Louis Cardinals fans. They had great players like Lou Brock and Bob Gibson, and we would act like we were them. We would play with a tennis ball, and a single would be hit in one area and a double in another and so on. We had all kinds of places set up where you would want to hit the ball.

Basketball was big for me as a kid too. I played a lot of basketball. I was a solid player and played a lot for Cheney, and we had some good teams. We made it to the state semifinals once. Another time we got beat in the opening round of the state tournament. I mentioned before that my dad could flat-out shoot the basketball, so I must have gotten some of that from him.

I played football in high school too. We didn't have high school baseball like they do now at most schools, but we played summer baseball. We had some pretty good teams. I was a decent baseball player and used to hit some home runs into the trees that lined the outfield. I recall a friend was in town once and heard me telling the trees thing and asked someone at the school about my home runs. I was telling the truth, and the guy told my friend, "Yeah, Jerry used to hit them out in the trees!" It was almost like we had rehearsed it.

We had a big rivalry with Garden Plain. The games against them were always big. Dad said the reason they were tougher than us was because the kids at Garden Plain drank beer and we drank milk. He used to say that all the time. Sometimes those Garden Plain kids would come over and see how tough the Cheney boys were, and we would fight and then go out together later. Those were the good times.

It was around that time in my life I got my first taste of chewing. We were about 14, and all the dads at our place that day decided to mess with their kids some. They had been chewing wintergreen Beech-Nut. And they were like, "Hey, do you guys want some of this?" Well, that sounded pretty good to us. "Yeah, sure, sounds good to us," we said. There were about three or four of us, and we all took some.

I put that old stuff in my cheek, and I will tell you what: I turned every different color that you have ever seen. I mean I puked and I was miserable and that was the last bit of chew that Jerry Kill ever put in his mouth.

I am sure glad my family was so tight with the Gordons, because I got to spend a lot of time with my good friend Brad Gordon, who died at the young age of 25. We had such a great time together. Brad was an exceptional person. I'm convinced he never had a bad day. He was one of those special people who enjoyed every minute of life. He always had a smile on his face, and everyone loved him.

I was coaching at Webb City, and Brad's parents were at our game when they got the call about Brad. He died of heart problems, far too young. It was just terrible. I remember he always carried a lot of small change on him, and at the funeral, we all put a little change—dimes, pennies, nickels—on his grave, and they remain to this day. I sure miss him.

I had many great friends in Cheney. We had a class of only 32 kids, and several of us were very close. There was Brad, Steve Scheer, Brian Bohm, Deena Dewey, Jana Compton, and me, and we were all thicker than thieves. No one dated each other or anything like that. We just had a good time together. The guys all played sports together, and we just hung around. It was such a small school that we also spent time with some of the older kids, such as Alan and Mark Scheer, Todd Rosenhagen, Brett Dewey, and many others. We were a bunch of good kids that had a good time together; I know they would die for me, and I for them. That's how it was and still is.

We went down to the river together, we hung around the Phillips 66 station together, we would go to concerts and rodeos together, and once we even went to the senior party at school when we weren't seniors. Another time, I recall driving all night to

Raton, New Mexico, to go to the horse races. I honestly believe we did what every other kid does, but we did it better!

When we were all together, we never did anything real bad. We never got in serious trouble or anything like that. I mean sure, we did a few things on Halloween like haul everyone's stuff from their yards out into the street and leave it there. But no one ever got mad. We never got in trouble for it. People just went out in the morning and picked it up.

We had a policeman in town called Smiley who always took care of us too. He didn't care if we did a little drinking, just as long as we didn't make a mess, picked up after ourselves. We used to cruise up and down the streets and show off for each other—just good, clean fun.

One story that stands out involves a wedding dance my friends and I attended. I can't even remember who got married. It didn't matter, because in those days in Cheney if there was a wedding, we just went. This was around the period of time when *The Blues Brothers* became famous. So we decided we were going to go to the dance as the Blues Brothers. Brett Dewey, Brad Gordon, the Scheer brothers, and I became the Blues Brothers.

We had to find some clothes. We went to the Salvation Army and were even digging in trash cans outside Walmart to get stuff. When we came into that wedding dance with our sunglasses on, well, it was really something. We always did crazy things like that, just having a good time.

I was always the kind of kid who had a lot of friends, and I thrived in groups. I remember when I got married, the cars were lined up 15 deep for the bachelor party. And afterward, many came to Mom and Dad's house to sleep. I mean we had people out on the lawn, everywhere! And I bet there were 500 people who attended the wedding dance. It was a great time! Like I said, I have always been around large groups of people. Maybe that's one of the reasons I have had success at building teams over the years.

When I look back I know that I really enjoyed my time in high school and college. School-wise, however, I wasn't the best of students, but for some reason I eventually got it all together, and my senior year in college I was an Academic All-American. I always thought that was pretty good for an old country boy from Cheney, Kansas.

Recently my mom said she wished I had done better in high school. I laughed and said, "Hey, Mom, look what I did in college. I mean, what are you saying? Have you got any proof of that?" "Well, no," she said. "I had your report cards, but we threw them all away when we cleaned out the garage." And I said, "But Mom, I graduated from college and did well." And she came right back at me and said, "I just wished you could have applied yourself a little better in high school." So I guess the bottom line here is that I wasn't a very good student in high school, but then when I got to college I got my act together. I wish Mom's memory wasn't so good. I'm still haunted by my high school record.

I mentioned before that in high school I was a pretty good basketball player, but I knew the only chance I had to play college ball was in football. I wasn't very big. I played football as a sophomore in high school at about 120 pounds, pretty small for collegiate football. (Later on in college I got my weight up to about 160 to 170 pounds and then gained some more before finishing up my college career.)

Getting recruited by any big school was not in the cards, so my high school coaches, Coach Thomas and Coach Disken, helped me get to Southwestern College in Winfield, Kansas. I got to play some as a freshman on the kickoff teams, which got me into the games. As a sophomore I split time with another guy, and then my last two years as a junior and senior I started and was a team captain.

I suppose academically I got my mind right in college and accelerated in my studies. I'm not exactly sure what I graduated with grade point–wise, somewhere above the 3.0 mark would be my recollection. My degree is in physical education, with a minor in biology.

I didn't really have what you would call a full scholarship, but I did have financial aid. I think I got about $500 for the scholarship and then the financial aid, which helped pay for my tuition. The extra money came from my jobs, plural. In college I worked three jobs. It was the only way to have any money. I worked at Wheeler's IGA grocery store, mostly stocking shelves and bagging groceries. In fact, when I retired from coaching, LeRoy Wheeler checked up on me to be sure I was okay. It really meant a lot to me, and I sure appreciated what he did. It was a good job at Wheeler's.

Another job I had at the time was making donuts at 4:30 in the morning at the campus café. My third job was delivering flowers. I was probably the only football player in the country who made donuts in the morning and delivered flowers in the afternoon. The jobs were fine, but the best part of them was that Rebecca, my future wife, worked at the IGA and the flower shop. So with her around, everything was wonderful.

I needed the money, so the three jobs helped, and I also played college football at the same time. My work ethic didn't all of a sudden hit me. That work ethic I talk about came from that small-town living, great values, and being surrounded by great people who affected my life. And having dad on my ass helped some too.

I wish I could have kept track of some of my high school and college friends a little better. I missed most of the reunions because of coaching football. And because of that, I have not been able to keep in touch regularly. It seems I am always running into somebody, though, and that keeps me somewhat connected.

When I go back to my hometown, I can walk through town and know everyone. Our school classes were small so we knew those that were a few years ahead or behind us grade-wise. Small towns have those kinds of advantages. I look forward to every time I get a chance to come home. I have my family there and all my friends, and I really relish the time I spend there.

I always believed there was something very unique about living in a small town. We learned small-town values that have stayed with us and, speaking for myself, have made me who I am today. Those great friendships from Cheney didn't come and go; they will be there forever. The only hurtful part is that Brad is not with us.

The connection with the people and the outdoors was how we got introduced to the country—these times with my mom and dad, my grandparents, my aunts and uncles, and my friends. And it all made Dad happy. As I look back, I know he loved watching my brother and me grow up and work hard. And I think some of Dad's proudest moments of his life were seeing his boys like he was as a youngster back in Elk Falls, Kansas. Life is different in a small town, and I miss it.

That's always been the life for my brother, Frank, too. (He would be plenty upset if I left him out of my book!) He's a good person and a straight-up guy. My brother and I did a lot together. We fished a bunch on the creek banks growing up. I mean my brother and I have pictures with my grandpa and these big stringers of fish. Basically we grew up on the banks. We set trot lines. You name it, fishing-wise, and we did it.

Like I said, my brother still lives in Cheney, and he has cattle and a lot of land, and I get out there with my boots on and that's me. I love to be with him and just kick around with him. Over the years, we have become closer and closer.

When we were younger we used to be very competitive. We used to get out and play basketball and he never could beat me, and it used to drive him absolutely nuts. We were both such competitors and wanted to win all the time, so it was really tough on him to lose to me, but I loved every minute of it. We were always fighting like cats and dogs over one thing or another. I mean we had some real battles.

Frank is a great inspiration to me. He took a different route in life than me and went to junior college. He is highly intelligent, but college was not for him. He stuck it out a whole two days and then quit. I recall him saying, "Nah, this is not for me." So he went to technical school. And he has so many skills. Frank can fix anything. Give him something that doesn't work and he can fix it. I can't fix a single thing, except broken-down football programs. I'm pretty good at that.

Frank also worked for Sears for a couple years and then started his own company, Killco Appliance. He works on washers and dryers, and he has been doing that for a number of years.

He eventually got married to Cindy, and they lived in an old farmhouse, saved their money up, and then built a nice home out in the country. Cindy is something. She is a pretty lady who can outwork any man I have ever seen, and she is a better hunter than Frank. I know he won't like it that I said it, but it is a fact. She can drive a fence post better than anyone in this country. I mean she is tougher than hell.

I know I can always count on my little brother. He has always been there for me, and actually he has kind of taken the place of dad in my life. If I need to ask him anything, like about money, for example, he has great advice for me. He is sharper than hell when it comes to money. Now that Dad has passed, I go to Frank for the same kinds of things I used to go to Dad to talk about.

He came up the hard way, I came up the hard way, and we busted our butts to get where we are today. And we learned all this from Mom and Dad. We have earned what we have gotten.

I used to laugh at him when he would come up to the big city for games. He hated the city. He used to tell me, "Look, you can have all this concrete jungle that you want, but for me, I'm going home." He would come to the bowl games and some of the big ones, but he used to say to me, "You are crazy. I don't know how you can do what you do with all the pressure and all the things people say."

And I would say back to him, "Well, just stay off the damn Internet and you won't know what people are saying."

The closeness that Frank and I have is very special. I think it was right after I got out of college that we really started to become close as brothers. We try to talk a couple times a week. With the football schedule I had, it was tough to get together, but we found a way. We go fishing, sometimes in Colorado, and just find the time to get together. He fishes and hunts turkey, deer, geese, and wild hogs. You name it and my brother hunts it. That's his passion. I used to do some hunting but now I haven't shot a gun in about 30 years because coaching has taken up so much of my time.

One thing our dad taught us was to give back to others, and Frank would give anything to anybody. He is that kind of guy. Frank will help out anybody who needs it. He has taken in kids and taken in families who needed his help. Frank would take in a dead dog if he thought it would help the dog out. Frank and Cindy were not able to have any children, so they have really taken to my kids. But Frank has also helped out so many other kids who have fallen on hard times. When his good friend Darin Compton died, he watched out for Darin's kids and actually had one of them live with them for a while. He has a big heart and has been there for a lot of people. The people in Cheney love him.

I always find it interesting how we take on our parents' traits. Mom came to the majority of my games over the years after my dad died, and it was great to have her around. She is like a caregiver with a heart of gold, always helping out people when she can. I am wired like my dad, but the kindness Frank and I have in our hearts today is from mom. The toughness comes from the old man. I can hear him saying, "You don't go around anything. You go after it and hit it head-on, man!"

It is probably how I have gotten myself in trouble from time to time, but I'm smart enough to know that coming in with that attitude is how we have been able to turn programs around. That's how the buildings have been built. My thought process is pretty direct: *This is how we are going to get this done, now let's go do it.*

Most people don't see my other side. People really don't understand behind the scenes of Jerry Kill. They don't see my closeness with the players, my coaches, my family, and things that I do that no one knows about. I should say some of that is Dad too, not all mom.

I just hope Dad would have approved of my decision to leave the game in 2015. I believe he would have told me, "You've got to do what you've got to do. I've got your back," but I'll never know. As I mentioned earlier, Dad is no longer with us.

When I was coaching in Michigan at Saginaw Valley State, we found out he had pancreatic cancer and was really sick. But even feeling the way he did, he came up to Saginaw Valley State to watch us play, and collapsed. I knew it was bad enough that I didn't think he would ever get out of Michigan. But I recall Dad saying, "I ain't dying in Michigan."

After dad collapsed, he spent some time in the hospital there. When he was ready to go home, Frank called Cessna to see if they could help out with the travel. They thought enough of Dad to send a private plane to get him home. The president of Cessna, Mr. Wallace, arranged the whole thing. "Jim Kill needs us, and we will be there for him," said Mr. Wallace. "He was one of the best employees we ever had." Dad never gave into his fight against cancer. He was so tough that after laying in that hospital bed for two weeks, when Cessna Aircraft arrived to fly him home, he got out of his wheelchair and walked to the plane. Some of his work friends were aboard, and he was not going to let anyone see him in a wheelchair.

Dad fought his cancer to the bitter end. He was not going to let it beat him. When he was in the hospital in Michigan, I would honor his request and sneak him a cigarette when Mom wasn't nearby. I probably shouldn't have done it, but I was not going to say no to Dad when he was dying. He kept up his battle through Christmas. I remember it was so important for him to see my girls, his two grandkids, so he just kept fighting.

Dad died a short time after Christmas. Tracy Claeys, one of my coaching assistants at the time and now head coach at Minnesota, was with us and around Dad near the end. One day, Dad said to Tracy, "Hey, Tracy, the keys are in the red coat." There was this old raggedy red coat out in the garage, and what he was referring to was that Tracy Claeys could come into his house at any time and he was welcome. It was simple: if Dad liked you, he told you about that old red coat. You wanted to be on that chosen list from Dad, and Tracy made it on the list.

At the end, I remember walking by Dad knowing it was probably going to be the last time I would see him. I hugged him, and he said to me, "I'm proud of you and I love you." And let me tell you, if you got those two things from Dad, it was special. I'll never forget it.

They came from everywhere to honor Dad at his funeral. He was so well known and liked by so many. It was a well-known fact that if you needed something, Dad would be there to help out. I was always proud to be his son.

I remember we buried him in his favorite blue jeans and a western shirt, just like he wanted it. We rolled a pack of cigarettes and put them on him the way he used to carry them. We had him wearing a Southwestern College ring and a Saginaw Valley State hat because that's the way we remember him. I know this for sure: when I go, if they put me in a suit and tie, someone is going to be in trouble. Just bury me like Dad and that will be fine with me. Just give me my blue jeans and a pair of boots, and that's the real Jerry Kill.

two

I'm a Football Coach

NO DOUBT IT TOOK SOME time before I realized what I wanted to do with my life. I wanted to be a football coach. Once I settled on it, the rest was easy. It seemed like it was a natural progression, because I loved the game so much.

One of my early high school memories—and not a good one, by the way—was when we were playing Garden Plain and my friend Steve Scheer and I got into our first varsity game. Our team was not doing well, and some of the older players were taking quite a beating, so Coach put us in. Excited as we were to get into the game, the excitement ended rather quickly when we got the living shit kicked out of us. It was quite the introduction to high school varsity football.

When I was younger, way back in Goddard, Kansas, and then later in Cheney, I played quite a bit of baseball. I had a pretty good stick and hit quite a few home runs. My brother, Frank, and I were very competitive from an early age. I mean we really went at it with each other.

I absolutely hated to lose, and so does my brother. I don't care if it was a high school game or playing marbles. I remember times when Frank would lose at Monopoly and he would get up and tip over the board, and I would sometimes do the same when I lost. I mean we would get up and throw the board and pieces from the game all over the place. I was four years older and should have known better, but I hated when he won at anything. And when he did, and it wasn't very often, I never knew what I might do.

We used to take a Nerf ball and go at it in some form of basketball, with a paper sack taped to the wall. And boy, did we go at it. I would beat him all the time, and he would run upstairs and tell Mom I was cheating. But let the truth be known: I just beat his ass up; it was as simple as that.

I always had that winning attitude. My competitive spirits were always extremely high. In some respects I think my competitiveness definitely increased as the years went by, and especially as I got older. I was a late developer.

Most of my successes playing sports really came in college. I think I surprised a lot of people, because when I played sports in high school, I was pretty small. In college, I got up as high as about 200 pounds, so there was quite a growth period for me during that short period of time. I am about the same now, but trust me, it's a different 200 pounds.

Once I developed, I was really strong, and in reality, my college years were probably the best years of my life from a physical standpoint. As a sophomore at Southwestern, I alternated with another guy at outside linebacker, and then when I was a junior, I became a regular. My senior year, I was also a team captain.

I recall playing a number of good games. The game really took off for me when Coach Dennis Franchione came on as head coach. He came from Kansas State. Coach Fran—that's what we called him—taught me a tremendous amount of football. I learned how to watch film and evaluate players. I mean, Coach trusted me a lot. He told me one time that I was the toughest player he had. I don't know if he was just trying to make me feel good or what, but I know this: it sure did make me feel good!

We became close as player and coach. If we had a player get in trouble, he told me to take care of it. As I said, he trusted me to do the right thing, and I would have done anything for the man. Later on, when I had trouble with my epilepsy, Coach made contact with me to be sure I was okay. That meant a lot, because I have such great respect for the man. With Coach Fran we won the first NAIA bowl game, the Sunflower Bowl at Southwestern. He was one great football coach.

I was one of those guys who was not the best talent in the world, but I was an intense competitor. I played my ass off every single game. I never took off a single down during a game or in practice. That's the way I am built. Letting up or not giving my best has never been an option for me. Dad instilled that in me.

I was very fortunate to play on some great teams with some outstanding teammates, especially in my junior and senior years under Coach Franchione. We were a pretty ornery bunch, maybe the most ornery group ever put together at Southwestern. We always had something going on together and were a really tight-knit group of guys. There are a lot of success stories that arose out of that group. I always had a good time, but I'll tell you what: During football season, I didn't mess around. I played football. We all did.

I was also involved in a ton of slow-pitch softball. I remember one time we took a group of guys and drove to a tournament in Hutchinson, Kansas. We were not far from Cheney, so all the guys stayed at my parents' house. We had driven a few vehicles up there, and there were 14 of us that stayed at my folks' place!

We didn't have any uniforms, and we were pretty raggedy looking. The other teams in the tournament had sponsors, great-looking uniforms, and all that expensive stuff, and we had nothing but 14 pretty good ballplayers. I mean, we were in T-shirts and jeans and cleats, and we each had a different-colored baseball cap on with a different team name on it. We did not look like much, but I'll tell you what: we could play ball.

We had a pitcher who was a real piece of work. He was far from a good-looking athlete, and we called him "Potbelly" Kelly. He could pitch and we could play, and we ended up winning the whole thing. I always remember thinking we were the image of the Bad News Bears, but all of us were pretty good college athletes. It was a good time and left me with many wonderful memories. We would play all afternoon, party into the evening, and then we'd come home and Mom would have all kinds of food ready for the group.

When I was in college, we did a lot of things like that. We used to play basketball on Sundays at a place called Cherry Street where they had eight-foot hoops, and we would organize teams among us and go at each other. It didn't matter if it was slow-pitch softball, basketball, or anything else, we knew how to compete.

Through all this I really became a hard-nosed, never-give-up competitor. The guys that I surrounded myself with knew how to play and wanted to win and compete, so it just made me want to win even more. And all this competitiveness, the winning-at-any-cost attitude, carried right with me into the coaching ranks.

Again, I have never handled losing very well. Losing is bad at all levels of competition, but the higher the level of competition, the more losing seemed to affect me. I remember when we lost a football game at Minnesota, it was like dying for an entire day. But I will say it was very difficult for me at every level. I handled it poorly.

I never wanted to let anyone down. In particular, I never wanted to disappoint my dad because we lost. I could not bear the thought that Dad might think I didn't work hard or coach hard. If we lost a football game, I felt like I let people down, and that to me was a very bad feeling. Losing was the end of the world for me at all levels. I guess I would have to say it was just as bad at Minnesota as it was at Southwestern, Midwest City High School, Saginaw Valley State, or at any place I have coached.

As I got older, there is no question that my competitiveness increased. Everybody that knows me will tell you, "Jerry Kill wanted to win at everything." As I went through the various coaching positions, my wife, Rebecca, can tell you that the way I reacted to things is likely why I'm out of coaching today. Winning was not an option, it was a necessity.

When we lost a football game and came home, I didn't want to be around anyone or talk to anyone; I just wanted to be left alone. I wanted to be by myself. I know it probably was not the right way to behave. It certainly was not the most respectful way to treat others, but I couldn't help it. Losing was too painful for me to accept.

After a loss, not only did I want to go off by myself but sleeping became impossible. I tried to figure out why we lost, what I could have done better. Why did we call this play or go with that defense? I would have this incredibly horrible feeling that I had let everyone down: my players, my coaches, and my dad. My brain would not shut down as I toiled over how I was going to "fix" what happened so it would never happen again. Because in my mind, I was not going to lose the next time. It was much too painful.

When Coach Franchione left Southwestern and went to Tennessee Tech, I helped out the new coach some. That following summer, '83, I got a job at Midwest City High School. I knew a couple guys that I had played with that were connected to the school, and that helped me get the job. This was unusual because, in Oklahoma, Kansas guys were not hired very often. Oklahoma guys got those jobs.

While at Midwest City I coached the linebackers and worked under legendary coach Dick Evans. (Dick Evans was a tremendous inspiration for me, because he won all kinds of football games.) And our quarterback was Mike Gundy, who is now head football coach at Oklahoma State. He was as good a baseball player as he was a football player.

They take their high school football seriously in Oklahoma. I recall the first game I coached was in front of 20,000 fans! I had a good time and learned some football and a little about coaching. It was a good beginning for me.

I was there for one semester and we had an exceptional team. I think we had six or seven Division I players on that team. From there I got a call from Coach Franchione—I was 23 years old at the time. He had been named the head coach at Pittsburg State in Pittsburg, Kansas. When he got the job, there were a couple coaches he didn't want to keep on his staff, but he didn't have the money to replace them, so he called me. And even though I was very young and with little experience, he asked me to come to Pittsburg State as his defensive coordinator.

He called and said, "Hey, do you want to coach some college football?" And I said—I was kind of lost for words—"Well, Coach, I mean…sure." He said, "I want you to come down here to Pittsburg State and be my defensive coordinator. It will be just until we get things figured out." I recall saying, "Coach, I'm awfully young for a job like that." And he said, "Well, I need you here."

Going into college coaching as a defensive coordinator was a pretty big step for a kid with zero college coaching experience. But Coach knew I knew the way he did business. And most important, he knew I had put in the time to study film to really know his defenses.

Joining his staff as a graduate assistant to coach the defense was a tremendous opportunity, but I made only $250 a month. When my dad and Rebecca heard what my salary was going to be, they both came close to having a heart attack. I mean, even back then you couldn't raise a family on $250 a month.

Rebecca and I moved into a small trailer house in Frontenac, Kansas, near Pittsburg. A friend of mine who had once lived with us when things weren't going so well for him, Doug Barto, owned the trailer. He and his dad both helped us out. It was kind of a nice payback for when we helped Doug.

Rebecca worked at a TV station and I coached football. The plan was for me to be a graduate assistant for the football team while filling the role as defensive coordinator and going to school. One day Coach pulled me out of class and said, "You need to do some recruiting." That ended the schooling part of my new coaching role.

Our team was very good, and we only lost a handful of games in the three years I was there. We made the playoffs every year and had some very good teams. Eventually they hired a defensive coordinator, because there was no question that I needed help, being a young coach and all. I switched over to coaching the linebackers, and Coach Lynn Meredith and I really worked well together. I needed help, and he provided it for me.

I was there for three years working under Coach Franchione, and I will say this about him: there is nobody, and I mean nobody, that works harder than Coach Fran. We would go to the office early in the morning and we didn't get home until late at night. He was a grinder. He covered everything in great detail and was involved in everything. Coach was super-organized—he was a great preparation guy—and had an unbelievable work ethic. I mean, you didn't get any days off. We worked and we worked, and he outworked everyone else. And that's why we won football games.

It was because of what Coach showed me, and all the wiring I had from my dad, that no doubt put me in that "grinder" category during my career as well. No doubt about it—I was, am, and very likely always will be a grinder.

Coach Franchione was a guy who came in and turned college football programs around. He turned the programs around at Southwest Texas State and New Mexico, and had a short but successful stint at TCU. Following those stops, he went to Alabama and on to Texas A&M. You don't go to those places and have success unless you are a good football coach. Coach Fran was unbelievable on game day. He taught me how to be a "game day" coach and all the important things about running a team. I learned so much from him in every aspect of the game. I mentioned TCU and I would be remiss not to mention here the success my close friend Gary Patterson has had there, becoming one of the finest, if not the finest, coaches in college football today.

I was soaking all this coaching wisdom in each and every day, but as a family we were struggling financially. On December 9, 1987, we had our first child, Krystal, which meant we had to stretch our dollar even further. We were in tough financial shape, no doubt about that. To top it off, Krystal was having some health problems and I had to find a way to make some money.

As it turned out, one of the linebackers I coached was the son of Tom Gosch, the athletic director at Webb City High School in Missouri. He knew of our family's financial situation and offered me the job as football coach at Webb City. As much as I hated to leave college football, I had to take the job for my family's well-being. I thought my days of coaching in college were over.

When I started there, I had the coaches come over from Pittsburg State to help us out during fall training camp, so it was easy to integrate the Pittsburg State systems. I coached the team like a college football team! When I was there we had an unbelievable run, and it continued after I left. In fact, there is a book, *Big Red Dynasty*, about the Webb City legacy. I coached the first Webb City team to win a state championship, in 1989, and I think they have won 12 more since then.

I had a great time at Pittsburg State and had the opportunity to coach many great young football players. I even coached a guy named Tom Beebe, whose son I ended up recruiting at Minnesota. There were a couple other guys, great players—John Roderique and Kurt Thompson—who both played for me and ended up coaching at Webb City and won a ton of championships. Because those guys went on to become coaches, the same systems we had at Pittsburg State still operate at Webb City High School.

At Webb City I taught four hours a day of weight-lifting classes and then I had an hour of study hall. I mean, I would not have taken the job if I didn't have that kind of setup. I had all our football guys in those weight-lifting classes, so it worked out well. We lifted weights all the time, even on game days. I had this old beat-up Ford Galaxy, and if a kid couldn't get to weight lifting, I would go get him. This car was like my dad's old truck. It was bad. I even had complaints when I parked it in front of the school. I drove a lot of kids over to weight-lifting classes, and we got bigger and stronger, no doubt about it.

My goal was to be bigger and stronger than anyone else. I went after kids everywhere. I scouted other teams, summer teams, and any place I could think of to find kids to play football. I recall going to a school wrestling match and there was a kid on Webb City's team who I thought looked tough when I first saw him. He was pretty small but had that look and swagger about him. He won his match, and I thought he would be good for our team because of his great competitiveness.

After the match I went up to him, complimented him on his win, and asked him outright, "What would it take for you to come out for the football team?" He looked up at me and said, "Coach, I'm on the football team." It must have been his size and my overextending myself that caused me to forget about him.

While at Webb City I had the chance to come in contact with one of the best administrators I have ever known, Ron Lankford. We formed a friendship to last a lifetime. Another great individual who became a lifelong friend was Rick Utter, a counselor at the school who has always been there for Rebecca and me over the years. Rick has a magnificent way of always providing good, sound advice, and I feel very fortunate to have had him in our lives for so many years. People like Ron and Rick and so many others provided the foundation for winning football games and guiding kids in the right direction.

I coached one of the best players ever to come out of Webb City, Mark Smith. Mark was 6'4" and weighed 215 pounds; he was the best two-way high school player I have ever seen. He started for me and was our sophomore quarterback when we won the state championship in 1989. Mark later went on to play at Arkansas.

We were on a roll in 1989 and had to beat St. Joseph to get to the championship game. The game was at St. Joe, and the wind was as strong as I have ever seen in a football game. We won the coin toss, and it is the only time I recall ever taking the wind at our backs to start a football game. We kicked off and held them, and they had to punt. The punt went 10 yards, and we took over and scored. We held them again, and their second punt actually went backward, and we scored again. Before anyone could blink twice, we had a 28–0 lead. It was a great win for us, and the wind provided an incredible early advantage. I will never forget it. We won 25 of 26 games that season and went undefeated in my last year.

We then went on to beat Sumner for the championship, and the fact is if we had played them 10 times, we probably would have lost 9 of them, but it was our day. After the state championship we paraded down Main Street and people came out of businesses and bars to cheer us on. It was without a doubt one of the better days of my whole life. I was so happy for our kids. I recall being carried all the way from the center of town up to the school. It was unbelievable. There was a band playing, and we were having the best time ever. I got up in front of everyone and did a little singing with the band.

They had a huge celebration that evening, and I can't begin to remember when we got home that night. But it didn't matter; we were state champs, and it was all worth it. It was the first championship that Webb City had ever won, and they have never forgotten it.

When I go back there, they always tell me I was the one that started the tradition of winning. And as I said, they have won a lot of football games since our first championship. The same traditions have remained. It was and still is a lot of blue-collar kids, mentally tough and full of that winning spirit. I was with John Roderique recently and asked him what his record is at Webb City since he became head coach. It is 236 wins and 20 losses. I mean, he is 236–20!

I am a pretty intense football coach with high expectations of our players, and at Webb City was no exception. We had one kid I recall who was a piece of work, let me tell you. Well, there was one day when he kept messing up a certain play that we were trying to run. I got frustrated and went over to him and yelled a few profanities at him and said, "Give me your damn helmet." I took it and put a bunch of dirt and grass in it and gave it back to him. I told him to put on the helmet and said to him, "Now, I have just given you some damn brains. Now go and use them!" In this day and age, I probably could not get by with behavior like that.

But those kids were something. I loved every last one of them. It was very tough to leave. There have been times over the years that I actually have reflected back and thought to myself, *Man, I should have stayed at Webb City because I am never going to have anything like that again.* I know I could have stayed and been happy.

Webb City was where I first learned how to rebuild programs. When I first got the job, I went to every boy in the school and told them, "Just give me a chance, and I will teach you how to play football and a little something about life too." That's how it all started. And then I would introduce them to the weight room and get them comfortable there. I would tell them they would be getting their bodies in shape and would be a spectacle for all the girls in the school. I said to them, "When you run out on that field, you will be something."

We had our own Bleacher Creatures. I bet we had about 300 of them, and they had their own seats at the game, got T-shirts made, and ran out on the field before the game, leading the football team out. It was really unbelievable! We had the cheerleaders, the pom-pom girls, and the band, and when we came out of that locker room, it was a sight. I mean, there was a line from the locker room to the field. No one had ever seen anything like that before, so it was quite the awakening for all the fans. And everyone got caught up in it.

We tried to include everyone; it was important to keep everyone involved. I believed in playing a lot of players during the games. I never wanted anyone to quit the team. Right from the beginning, we started winning. Kids would come in early to watch film and just hang out with the team. They were involved in something special, and they didn't have anything else to do. The best part of most of their lives was school, and football was a big part.

We had a kid named Gene Stanley, and Gene didn't get to play a lot, but he was a member of our football team just like everyone else. We had this one game where we were way ahead, and the team started yelling at me, "Come on, Coach, put Gene in the game! Put Gene in!" It was kind of like the movie *Rudy*, when the players all start yelling, "Rudy, Rudy!"

So I put him in, and I looked down and noticed he had his shoes on the wrong feet. It was so funny, and everyone was laughing, but Gene went down the field and made the tackle. People went absolutely crazy. I made him the Special Teams Player of the Week! He got a picture from the team and an award.

We had another kid who was a foreign exchange student from France by the name of Jerome Tarting, and he didn't know one thing about football. We kind of did the same thing for him that we did for Gene Stanley. We put him in late in the game, and he didn't have a clue what to do. He didn't even know what the white lines on the field were all about.

The other team was running the football, and the kid with the ball went out of bounds. He was almost to the bench when Jerome absolutely obliterated him. I mean, this exchange student clobbered him—as flagrant a foul as probably has ever been in the history of the game. The head coach of the other team went crazy, and I had to talk with him after the game to explain. I apologized and said, "Hey, Coach, that kid is from France. He doesn't know a thing about the game or the rules. I'm really sorry."

It definitely was hard to leave that great school and those wonderful kids. I mentioned the superintendent, Ron Lankford, earlier, and I always give him a hard time when I see him. I tell him, "You are the only one who ever fired me." He told me one day, "Jerry, you belong coaching college football. With the way you coach and with your work ethic, college football is where you belong. What you have done here is never going to happen again, so move on to the college game." Not long after that, I went back to Pittsburg State and the collegiate ranks again. I always kid Ron, saying, "It's never going to happen again? Webb City has rarely lost a game since I left!"

Here's how I found my way back to Pittsburg State: Coach Chuck Broyles, who was at Pittsburg State then, came over to my study hall class at Webb City one day and said, "Coach, I would like to have you come with me to Pittsburg State and be my offensive coordinator. You're the guy we want. Do you want the job?"

My first thought was this would be my chance to get back to college football. I had been the defensive coordinator there, so being the OC was a great opportunity. My experience on both sides of the ball was likely to open up even more coaching opportunities down the road.

There was a kid I had coached who was now coaching over there, and there were other coaches whom I had coached with before, so I knew it would be a good fit. And Coach Broyles was a great guy. Chuck was exceptional with player relations, and the players just loved him. So I committed to going back to Pittsburg State.

Two days after I had accepted the job, Coach Franchione, who had left earlier to go to Southwest Texas Sate, called me and offered me the defensive coordinator job with him. It put me in quite a dilemma. What was I going to do?

But the decision was ultimately an easy one to make. I had always learned from Dad that your word is one of the most important things you have in life, and loyalty is right there with it. I had already promised Coach Broyles I would go with him. I went back and forth as to what I should do, but when it came to decision time, I went with what I was taught. Once you make the commitment, you have to stay with your word.

Coach Franchione was pretty disappointed in me. I remember when I told him, he voiced his displeasure, and when we hung up the phone, I teared up. It hurt. It really did. I didn't want to let him down. I could have very well taken that job with Coach Fran, but I felt it wasn't the right thing to do. And as I already mentioned, I wanted that experience on the other side of the ball that I could get with Coach Broyles.

It worked out, that's for sure. We ended up playing for the national championship twice and winning it once. Our record back then was amazing. We had some phenomenal football teams. All we did was win. We expected to win, and our kids expected to win. When you win a national championship, you feel it for a lifetime.

I remember before the title game I was looking closely at our opponents during warm-ups. They looked awesome. They were big, fast, and really filled out their uniforms. I went over to Coach Broyles and said, "Coach, look at those guys over there. They are pretty good-looking players." Coach Broyles looked at me and said, "Jerry, my boy, they can only put 11 of them on the field at one time, and they will go against our best 11. And our best look pretty good too!"

When we won it, we owned the town. We were in a position to do anything we wanted to do. The town was so appreciative and so happy; Pittsburg, Kansas, was in a state of joy. I recall Coach saying, "Should we go out with the donors tonight or with the players?" And every single one of the coaches yelled out, "Let's go with the players!" We all ended up at the same place, and it was a great time. I will never forget it.

We had great players, and their relationships and friendships are special. We had five players who made it to the National Football League, so that gives you an idea of the caliber of players we had. Ronnie West and Ronnie Moore were a couple of them, and we had so many others—great players and great individuals. I couldn't begin to start naming them, because the list would go on forever.

I loved the job at Pittsburg State University, which has the only gorilla mascot among college football teams in the nation. And our football teams were fierce and tough like our mascot. When we came onto that football field, the gorilla mentality and toughness was with us. We had great players and great coaches too. I had John Roderique on my staff, and my old friend from college, Anton Stewart, coached the defensive line. We had a great group.

I was having the time of my life, and I got real used to winning. Every place I had been we had won. We expected to win, and it carried with me to wherever I went. The program at Pittsburg State had been broken, and Coach Fran had fixed it on my first stop there. I was a part of rebuilding that program, and that will always stay with me. You cannot have much more fun coaching football than winning. And we got a good taste of it.

And then I got the opportunity to become a head football coach at Saginaw Valley State. I was on the Glazier Coaching Tour teaching option football. It was a big-time coaching clinic tour, and I was on with some great coaches. There were about three or four of us that taught option football.

People like Frank Solich and Tommy Tuberville were there. It was through this program that I got to meet so many coaches from all over the country. We went from the East Coast to the West Coast to the Midwest, and I was around both college and high school coaches. I got to know practically everyone in the coaching ranks talking on the split back veer offense.

During one of our stops in 1994, I was speaking in Detroit, Michigan, and there was a guy there watching me speak. The speech was in front of some very high-powered high school coaches. When I got done speaking, I was told this guy had made a call on my behalf.

Soon after, Bob Becker, the athletic director at Saginaw Valley State, called me and said he wanted to have some time to talk with me. I went to his house and visited with him. They offered me the head coaching job at Saginaw Valley State. Rebecca and I talked it over and thought it was the right decision to move on.

Saginaw Valley State had not had a lot of success. I think my salary was about $42,000 a year, and I didn't have a big budget to hire coaches. I took a guy named David Wiemers with me. I knew his dad from high school coaching, and we had been together at Pittsburg State. We got ourselves a Ryder truck and we took off together for Saginaw, Michigan—just the two of us—to begin building a football program. I give David a lot of credit for getting our coaches together there.

When we got there, we stayed in this old hotel and started the program from scratch. I had a little money for coaches and I hired a guy named Chris Holgard, who has gone on to do very well in the financial business. Chris had been with Rocky Hager at North Dakota State. Rocky had run the split back veer, so he knew what I wanted to do at Saginaw Valley State.

David became our defensive coordinator and I took the role as offensive coordinator, even though I was the head coach. Then we hired Eric Klein. I brought him on board because of Gerald Young, who recommended him. Gerald is now the athletic director at Carleton College in Minnesota and a great friend of mine. We went to college together at Southwestern and have been close friends ever since.

I remember hiring Eric for about $22,000 a year, and he was like only 21 years old. He came in for the interview, this super-smart kid from Carleton with an earring in his ear. It didn't matter, because I knew I was going to hire him. The interview went well, and I told him he had the job. I added a little side note: "Hey, by the way, you need to have that earring out when you come back to work." We still laugh about that to this day.

We had another guy who came from Pittsburg, by the name of Del Fuchs, and he wanted to volunteer along with Dave Pettyplace and Mike Sullivan. Dick Horning and Todd Adams had been there and they stayed with us. We had some others join us and overall put a good group together. Rob Reeves ended up being our starting quarterback, even though he didn't start our first game. He came into the game and had great success and became an outstanding option quarterback. Rob later coached with me until I retired.

It didn't take us long to get back on track. We had winning records every year I was there, and we were nationally ranked my final two years there. We were successful in creating a winning environment and got a lot of people to start attending our football games. We recruited hard and got some real good kids. I was told when I arrived, "Don't think you are going to win here, because it just isn't going to happen." We proved the naysayers wrong.

It was at Saginaw Valley State that Tracy Claeys joined my staff. David Wiemers was a real good friend of Tracy's, and David told me, "Hey, Coach, I got this friend who is a high school coach, and I know it won't be expensive to get him. He is a great coach and he can live with me up here."

So that's how we got Tracy to coach our defensive line. And Tracy stayed with me a long time, more than 20 years, and he is now the head football coach at the University of Minnesota.

Our big rival in the league was Brian Kelly, who is now head coach at Notre Dame. Matt Limegrover was an assistant coach at Ferris State at the time. They beat us and were really good in the offensive line, and when I eventually was hired to coach Emporia State, I was able to get Matt to come with us. And Matt is another coach who stayed with me for many years, and he is now at Penn State.

Bob Becker, as I mentioned, was the athletic director and was one of the best guys I have ever been around. I loved the guy. We had a great relationship. He treated us all great. When Bob retired, I was appointed athletic director along with being the football coach.

We had the Detroit Lions come to Saginaw Valley State for their training camp. Bobby Ross was the head coach then, and they had Barry Sanders at the time, along with other great players. Barry was from Wichita, Kansas, so we knew all about him. And Bobby Ross, he came to Saginaw and we spent a lot of time together. When he decided to bring the Lions training camp to Saginaw Valley State, it was a great thing for the college and our budget, plus we learned a few things watching them practice.

One of the first things we did at Saginaw Valley State was go after a better weight room. I remember going to Bob Becker and telling him I was fond of another room and thought it would better serve us as a weight room for the team. And he told me, "Well, go ahead then."

That night we moved all the equipment in. I mean, when we got the go-ahead on something, there was no time to waste. We got it done and got it done right then. And boy did it look good with what we had. We were all set to get to work.

The next day Bob came up to me and said, "You moved into the new weight room already? Well, did I get my ass chewed out because of you." I said, "Why is that?" And he said, "This is a union school. You can't just move like that!" I replied, "Well, you told me to go ahead." And he just laughed and said, "Don't worry, I got your back. But I learned one thing about you, Coach Kill, and that is don't ever tell you anything that I have to work out the details on first, because I now know you are going to go and just do it, and I mean right now!"

Bob was an A+ human being. He gave me my start as a head coach, and to me he was like another father and a big brother. He trusted me. He knew what I was about and saw the long hours that we would work, and I know in his heart he felt, *Damn, this guy is serious about what he is doing.* And he backed the team and me all the way. He was a great leader and a huge part of my life. Bob has passed away now, and I miss him.

I talked before about living the dream. Well, this was it. We had some great football teams and won a lot of games. There was one game where we ran the football for more than 600 yards!

One of the biggest things that happened to us from an adversity standpoint was when we were getting ready to play Brian Kelly and his Grand Valley team for the championship. We had to have this game.

A few weeks before the championship game, I received a call from home that Dad had cancer and was given only six months to live. It was devastating news. But he had been doing pretty good and came up to Saginaw Valley for the game. We had been practicing all week, and Dad seemed to be doing all right.

Then on a Friday night my mom got ahold of Bob Becker and he came to see me at the football field and said, "You need to get back to your house as soon as possible. Your dad is in really bad shape."

I let one of my assistants take over practice and frankly wasn't sure what to do about Dad. I didn't know any doctors in the area, but one of our donors named Bob Loftus helped us out. His wife was a nurse at Saginaw Hospital, and she met us at the hospital and got everything arranged for us. Dad was absolutely yellow-looking and needed some immediate care. The problem was they needed to do surgery the next day to put a stent in, and that was Saturday, the day of our big game against Grand Valley.

The game was at 11:00 AM; we were playing for the championship and dad was having surgery. And I didn't know what to do. I was really torn until Mom said to me, "You know what your dad would want you to do."

I mean, I thought Dad might die. How could I go to the game? And then Dad looked up at me from that hospital bed and said, "You get your ass to that game!" And so I went to the game, and we had the game won except for a freshman running back fumbled the ball at the end, which allowed Grand Valley to take the ball down the field and beat us. It was a pretty tough way to lose. Dad died later on at home, as I mentioned, and it was one of the toughest times of my life.

I was doing well at Saginaw Valley State, but when I was at Pittsburg State, the athletic director at Emporia State was always trying to hire me to coach there. This was before my dad passed away. Emporia State had a job opening again, and what was going on with my dad was a story that most knew about. So the AD at Emporia State called me and said, "Let me tell you something. We just lost our coach, and this would be a great reason for you to come back and be close to your mom." He offered me the job, and I took it. It was a good decision. I got to be near Mom.

My time at Emporia State was a good two years. I got to see Mom and my brother quite often and I wasn't all that far from home. At the beginning it was one of those same kinds of things where I had to leave my family and head over there to get things started. I mean I was living in a dormitory at the beginning. It was about three to four months before I saw Rebecca and the kids again. The kids were in school and we just could not all move at the same time.

The transition at Emporia State was going pretty well, and then we got some bad news about one of our players. Our graduate assistant came over and told me, "Coach, Brian Wagner is in bad shape. A bunch of guys kicked his head in, and he is in serious condition. He is being flown to Wichita to the hospital there."

It was one of those things where he had been beaten badly and was basically brain-dead. It was the first time I had ever seen a machine turned off on a patient. His parents were there, and it was just absolutely terrible. It is a memory that I will sadly never forget.

We took the whole team to the funeral and I spoke there, but what are you supposed to say? It was such a difficult time, just unbelievable. I hadn't been on the job a month when that happened. It was a very rough start at Emporia State.

Our athletic director who hired me retired, and our new athletic director—Kent Weiser, who is still there—came in. He treated me so well and was another one of the great athletic directors I worked for.

I told him we needed new offices and we needed this and that in order to win. We had to do some things quickly to get caught up with Pittsburg State. So I can absolutely guarantee you we were the only team in the world that would get boosters to buy in as fast as they did. I met with this group of about five or six and said, "This is what we need to do to beat Pittsburg State," and they were on board and ready to go.

We did our weight room and got new offices and lots of other stuff, and I think we got it all done in four months. We were in and ready before we played a game that year. We were building a program and we had to sell our mission to them. I was there two years and we were not real good, but the program foundation was being built.

It was at that time that I began to put together my coaching staff that stayed with me for a long time. Matt Limegrover joined me at Emporia State, and Tracy was already with me. Rob Reeves came, and David Wiemers was there. So it was the beginning of a nucleus of guys who stayed with me for a long time. Eric Klein was with me also, and we started building the group that would soon be going with me to Southern Illinois.

I expected to be at Emporia State for a little longer than just the two years. But that was the case in the other places I had coached as well. I had gotten to know a lot of people, and those connections and the experiences I was getting put my name out there for schools that were looking for head coaches. I never planned ahead with my moves; they just seemed to come about for a variety of reasons.

When I was at Saginaw Valley State, we played in the Great Lakes Intercollegiate Athletic Conference and there was a guy in it named Dave Coffey. Dave had been the assistant athletic director when Coach Franchione was at Tennessee Tech, so we knew each other some and had a lot of mutual friends. I guess he figured by seeing us enough that, "These guys can coach football. They can turn programs around."

He made a call to Paul Kowalczyk, the athletic director at Southern Illinois. Paul had been at Kansas State and Northwestern during their turnarounds. He got in touch with me and said, "I want you to come and interview to be the head football coach at Southern Illinois. We are looking for a guy to come in here and turn this program around."

Dave Coffey had told him, "Jerry Kill is the guy to turn your program around from losers to winners. You do not need to call anyone else. Jerry is the guy!"

Now, I didn't know one single thing about Southern Illinois. So I said, "Well, I need to talk with my athletic director, but sure, I'll talk with you about the job."

I did a little research, and my first thought was, *Why would I want to do that?* They had not won in forever. The same time as this was going on, Coach Fran was going to be head coach at Alabama, and Gary Patterson, who was a good friend of mine, was going to TCU. And Gary called me and wanted me to come with him to be his offensive coordinator at TCU.

So I was in a tough spot. I could go to TCU with Gary, and there was a good possibility Fran might ask me to go to Alabama. I can recall thinking, *What the hell am I supposed to do?* I mean, Alabama or TCU...or Southern Illinois University?

Truth be known, at that time I really wanted to go to TCU with Coach Patterson. But I had all these coaches who I had hired to come with me to Emporia State, and they hadn't been there long enough to where one of them would get my job. At least we couldn't really count on that happening. I wanted to protect my coaches, and I knew I could take them with me if I went to Southern Illinois as the head coach.

And then Coach Fran told me, "You know, Jerry, you are never going to get a big-time head coaching job because of all the small schools you have been at. What you are going to have to do is take on a program that is truly broken and then fix it to make a name for yourself."

And that's how I ended up at Southern Illinois University as the head football coach.

| three |
On to Illinois and Minnesota

BEFORE I TOOK THE JOB at Southern Illinois University, as I mentioned, I had several other coaching opportunities, and I had asked myself, *What the hell am I supposed to do?* After I had first taken the job and was getting acquainted with the football program at Southern Illinois University, I can recall asking myself many times over, *What the hell did I do?* I mean, this program was absolutely unbelievable!

When I went down to look at the football program, I arrived in the evening, and Paul Kowalczyk, the athletic director, showed me around in the dark. The facilities were absolutely pathetic! They were the worst. The indoor practice dome at Minnesota doesn't even compare to what I was seeing. I had never seen anything like it. There was nothing even to compare to what I was looking at. It was that bad.

The weight room was about the size of a bedroom, and it was filthy dirty. The locker room was about a quarter the size of that at Minnesota. The stadium press box was an old trailer that had been put up above the stands some time back. I have to say that again because I still do not believe it even after seeing it: the press box was an *old trailer* that had been put up above the stands some time back! Underneath the stadium everything was rusty and dirty. I actually thought the whole stadium might fall down. The turf on the field was about 30 years old and as hard as a rock.

Over the years as I have told others about my arrival at Southern Illinois, I have been asked many times, "Why did you take the job after the first impressions you had?" At first I was doing everything I could to talk myself out of the job as I saw more and more. It was a nightmare. However, I could recall Coach Fran telling me that in order to get a big-time college job with my background, I was going to have to take a broken program and fix it. At Southern Illinois, I could honestly say there was no question it was broken, but in the beginning I wasn't sure it was fixable.

Paul saw the same thing I was seeing when he took me around and must have known what I was thinking, because he said to me early on in the process, "Hey, Coach, stick around one more day."

Before anything was final, I had a visit with the school president, Dr. James Walker, who had been at Middle Tennessee when they took that program to Division I. That was his vision, and he told me, "We are going to get this right here." He sold me, and I grabbed the bait. Dr. Walker was a great man to work for, and I supported his mission.

So we took off for Southern Illinois University. I had met with Rebecca and the girls, and we had talked about it at length. It was another tough decision because it meant moving again. It was especially hard on the girls to move because they had developed friends, were playing softball, basketball, and soccer, and loved where we were living in Emporia.

My mom told me, "I was pretty sure you were going to do this anyway, because you have to go chase your dreams. You have to do what your dad would want you to do. Go chase your dreams."

I was the new head football coach at Southern Illinois University. I took the coaches with me from Emporia State and then added

Pat Poore, Brian Anderson, Jay Sawvel, and Travis Stepps. We put together a great group at SIU, and we were ready to go after it.

When my assistant coaches showed up at Southern Illinois to coach with me, the common question among all of them was, "What the hell has he gotten us into in this place?" They were in total shock. They were seeing what I had seen, and they couldn't believe it!

The program was just plain dead. We had players who should not have been wearing a football uniform. We had players get picked up for cocaine possession. The weekend after our arrival, we had more players in trouble and we had to go in there and clean house.

But the great stories about the beginning of my tenure at SIU are not about the players at the time but about the coaches. It was the time when we began to form the staff that stayed with me for a long time. They knew how to do their jobs and get things done.

People like Tom Matukewicz, who is now the head coach at Southeast Missouri State, went with me to Southern Illinois, along with the others that I previously named. They were all exceptional coaches, and they all had their work cut out for them, big time.

My coaches and I initially had nowhere to live and found a place to stay on campus. It was awful. The heat didn't work. It was snowing and freezing cold outside, and there was ice everywhere. We finally were able to get some money and found a place to stay with four of us to a room, which was better than what we'd had. I'm sure many times my coaches must have thought, *What the hell are we doing? Are we absolutely nuts?*

It was unimaginable but we stayed together and became a very close staff. There was a lot of bonding going on. We would go to the Schnucks grocery store, and we took turns cooking and doing everything together. We became a football coaching staff and friends for life.

While in town one day we met this lady, Laverne O'Brien, at the grocery store. She kind of took us all in and we became "her boys."

She was about seventy years old, and we were like her kids. One of the things she told us was that we better be in church on Sunday. So she became a part of our group with church and everything else that was going on.

At SIU my coaches and I didn't even have offices. We had cubicles. Cubicles! We didn't have computers, and when we did get some, we had to do all the wiring and everything ourselves. Because of some union issues, we weren't supposed to do any of the wiring, but we were told, "Go ahead and do it yourself; just don't tell anyone." So Tom Matukewicz worked at it all night and got it up and running. Tom made it work for us.

When we recruited players, we didn't even take them to the stadium, and some other places, because if we had, they would never have gone there! I mean *never*. That's how bad it was. You would have to have been nuts to want to go there. But we turned it around with a lot of hard work and by eventually getting the right players to go to SIU.

What we did there was hard to believe. We had a group of guys who came in together, and we worked our tails off. I'm not sure we always knew what we were doing, but we started to win in our second year. Everywhere else we have been, we started winning in the third year, but at SIU we started to turn it around the second season.

We won with the worst facilities possible. In fact, I am stretching it to call what we had facilities. Paul Kowalczyk supported us to the end. He never cut our budget even when there was a huge deficit to make up. He believed in us and what we were doing, and I am forever thankful to Paul. And Paul deserves a lot of credit here, because at a time when he was forced to overcome huge deficits, his basketball and football programs still won.

We got that program rockin' and rollin', and people in the area will tell you it was the best seven-year run in Southern Illinois University history. When things looked really bad in the beginning, I told the staff, "It's all we got, and we can't do anything about it at the moment, so let's make it work!" And we did. And to this day, Paul Kowalczyk will say to anyone what we accomplished with SIU football was "the greatest football story that has never been told."

I don't like excuses. I never have. I just take on any obstacle in my way. Dad taught me that. The problems were not only on the football field, in the locker room, and inside the bad facilities; they were everywhere. I didn't even have a car in Southern Illinois. And no one was willing to help us out because the previous coach had alienated people so badly. So I went to a local car dealer and bought a vehicle and became friends with the owner, Jim Hayes, who later gave me a vehicle to use.

Everything seemed to be going against us in the beginning. At the first team meeting, we walked into a brawl between players. When I said we had to fix and change *everything*, I wasn't kidding. Things were a real mess, and we had to clean them up.

On top of everything else, it was so hot that even the Florida kids could hardly stand it. It got up to more than 100 degrees. And there was this digital thermometer near the field that showed the temperature, and I told somebody to shut the damn thing off. It was hot enough that we didn't need to be reminded of the temperature. We had sometimes 10 or 11 kids at practice going down because of the heat. We had a lot of work to do.

We did everything we could for an advantage. I mean we even worked to get lights on the field to make it more attractive for our fans. We had everyone helping out, including the union and the president and so many others. And when we got those lights, it was something. We called the first night game Hawgs and Dogs, and we had motorcycles all around the field. And when we came out and they cranked them up, let me tell you, we were ready for a ballgame. Someone asked me once after I told them the story, "Did you win the game?" My answer was, "What do you think?"

We worked hard at every practice. We coached and our players worked, and eventually they started to believe in what we were doing. I remember one of our players, Tony Rinella, was doing something wrong in practice. I forget what it was he did, but I told him, "Get over to that hill and run your ass up and down until I get tired of watching you!" And he did. And I forgot about him!

We went through our practice, and he kept going up and down that hill. Finally one of the guys came over and said, "Hey, Coach," and I said, "What do you want?" And he said, "Rinella is still running the hill." It was like 40-some minutes he had been running. So I yelled over to him, "Hey, Rinella, get your ass back over here!"

So he came back over to practice, and the next day our equipment guy, Alvy Armstrong, got some paint and he painted RINELLA HILL right there where Rinella had been running. From then on when someone didn't do something the right way or screwed up something, all I had to do was point, and they went over to run Rinella Hill.

We had some outstanding teams at Southern Illinois, but I have to mention one guy who really helped out the team. And this guy is a legend not only at Southern Illinois University, where he played in the 1960s, but also for the 30-plus years he played and coached in the National Football League. His name is Carl Mauck.

Carl came to us and coached the tight ends the last two years I was at SIU. He is one of the most unique individuals I have ever known. He came off as this tough guy that would appear to be hard to get along with, but I'll tell you what, the players and coaches all loved him. He was a great addition to our football team.

He had been let go by the San Diego Chargers, and not only had he been a great player and coach for so many years but he was the last guy who ever snapped the ball for Johnny Unitas, the former Hall of Fame quarterback. I mean, this guy used to be the center and snapped the ball for the great Johnny U. Unbelievable!

Carl at one time played for legendary coach Bum Phillips, and Carl was Bum's guy. He was a great player and coach, and after his NFL coaching career ended, he showed up here at Southern Illinois and didn't have a job. He came and worked free for us for two years.

After spending all those years playing football and coaching in the NFL, it was obvious he knew something about the game. To this day, those who coached with Carl will tell you Carl Mauck made us all better coaches. He was a strong influence on the players and on every one of us.

When we beat Indiana at their place, Carl stood up in front of our SIU fans and led us in fight songs with tears running down his face. You could be in the business for a lifetime and you would never meet a more competitive dude than Carl Mauck. I'm lucky to know him and fortunate that he came my way. Carl Mauck is the real deal. He has become a wonderful friend and confidant.

Carl used to keep a daily journal on our team at SIU while he was on my staff. Here are a few excerpts from two seasons at Southern Illinois with the great Carl Mauck:

August 14, 2006: Our 7:00 AM, stretch got rained out. We have a double practice today. Our first practice was hot, and it was mostly individual, but we did have a blitz drill, and it was good. We practiced in the AM and got rain in the PM and waited and then practiced mostly team. It was good. The old man had a burr under his ass. He loves football and doesn't like people who don't want it as much as he does. I know the feeling. It is the reason he has done a good job at SIU, and he does it on a shoestring. He has good assistants and they have done a good job for him.

August 24, 2006: We had a good practice today. There was a good fight between Marquez and Wims, and Coach Kill got decked. It was on his birthday.

August 30, 2006: We had a walk-through at the stadium. They at least tried to paint it. It was like putting a blue ribbon on a cow turd. Coach Kill sat down in the offensive conference room and talked to me about how it will be good to get between the lines on game day. He didn't think he would get a chance back last spring because of his cancer. He is a tough nut and has been good for the school because he puts the students first.

September 16, 2006: We played Indiana and won 35–28 and won for the first time ever vs. a Big Ten team. We started slow and were down 14–0 but came back and scored before the half to make it 14–7. We then scored 28 points in the second half. The QB had a good day, and if we can play at that level, we will be tough to beat. It was a very emotional win for everybody. I had three college teammates at the game, and it was great to have them there. My brother, Dr. J.R. Mauck, was also there, along with about 400 Salukis fans. It was a great day to be a Saluki.

October 22, 2006: I went to 8:00 Mass, and after Mass Matt Limegrover called and said Coach Kill had another seizure and was in the hospital. It was a tough day after that. We met with the players and told them and gave them the day off till Monday night at 7:00 PM.

October 23, 2006: We game-planned all day and worked well. It was strange not having Coach Kill around. We met with the players at 7:00 PM and then finished up. We made some front calls that were not right in the game, and it probably cost us. We worked to get it corrected with the QB, line, and tight ends.

October 24, 2006: We practiced and it was the best practice in weeks. We were sharp. The QB was sharp and on time with the routes. It was good all through practice. Monday night I saw Coach

Kill and asked him if he wanted me to comb his hair, and he said he would piss on my grave, so I know he is getting better.

December 9, 2007: I flew back after the game. I went to Carbondale and graded the film and packed my little space and left. I will always remember my two years at SIU. I told Ted Cunningham, my former teammate, that I wanted to give the Salukis two years, and I did. I want to thank Coach Kill for giving me the chance to help my school and to get some of my dignity back after leaving the NFL. I want to thank the assistant coaches who are all good men for letting me help them. Jerry Kill and his band of coaches cared about their players and made them men who were achievers who will go far in life because they paid the price of sacrifice and hard work.

Anytime I have ever had any trouble in my life, whether it is health-related or I just need someone to listen, or whatever I need, I go to Carl Mauck.

I have so many stories about my SIU football team and the great coaches, players, and other people I was around there. I remember walking off the field one day during our first year. Our record at the time was 1–10 losses, and Mike Reis, our play-by-play announcer, came up to me and said, "Coach, how are you doing? Are you doing all right?" And I said, "Hell no, I'm not doing all right." And he said back to me, "Well, you said you were going to come in here and turn this thing around," and we just laughed. And then he looked at me and said, "I'll tell you what you need to do." And I said, "What's that?" And he said, "You've got to get better players." I looked at him and said, "No shit!" And he said, "Better players make you a better coach!" I will never forget that. He was right, and I knew it, because you can coach all you want, and if you don't have the players, you are not going to win.

Just recently I was with Mike at a Southern Illinois University basketball game, and the Salukis were not doing very well. I looked over at Mike, who is also the basketball play-by-play guy, and said, "Maybe what they need is a better play-by-play guy doing their games!"

We worked hard to get those better players Mike was talking about, and we brought football back at Southern Illinois University. We had a great contact at Coffeyville Junior College in Dickie Rolls. He really took care of us by sending some great players our way.

After we had cleaned some house and got some of our own recruits in, we found a nucleus of kids who wanted to win. We had some tough kids, great running backs, great linemen, and the whole group became something very special. We hit the jackpot with the kind of kids we brought in and developed as football players.

I want to especially mention one kid who was at SIU named Bart Scott. Because of disciplinary reasons, Bart wasn't even on the team when we got there, but he wanted to play. I told him I didn't care about the past, and if he wanted to play, he was welcome. It was the beginning of a great relationship, and let me tell you, Bart Scott was one great football player and an even better person. He proved that by having a very successful career in the National Football League, and he is now with CBS as a football analyst. Bart and I continue to have a great relationship, and I am very proud of what he has accomplished in his life.

Another player I want to mention is Joel Sambursky, who was one of our quarterbacks. I don't want to start leaving names out here, but Joel needs mentioning. This kid, pound for pound, was as tough as they get. I always talk about being a hard worker and having mental and physical toughness; well, Joel Sambursky is the poster boy for those accolades. We remain friends today, and he is my financial adviser. I trusted him with the ball when I was his coach, and now I trust him with my finances. He is another, like so many, that I am so proud of and proud to call my friend.

Whenever we beat one of our opponents we had a graveyard where we symbolically buried them. We would do that because when I took the job at SIU, it was well known that the school was a graveyard for its past coaches. My assistants and I were told there was no chance to win at SIU. We proved them wrong! But it wasn't only the winning; the new facilities we made happen helped too. And they are incredible. There is a great new stadium, new offices, a new weight room, and everything you would ever want. And yes, the old press box trailer is gone too, with a wonderful new press box in its place.

Success didn't come about just from the players and the coaches on the field. There were so many amazing people behind the scenes. We had some great support staff, like Sharon Lipe, my administrative assistant, who did about everything for me. And her husband, Roger, was our team chaplain. They are both just great people. And Tracy Wiseman was another who did so much for us and was such a special person. They were the best. They have helped me through so much of my life. They used to say when I walked in, "Here comes the tornado from Kansas."

With all that was happening, we also brought in the community. Our attendance was up and the great people of southern Illinois fell in love with our football team.

With all our winning and finally getting things on track at SIU, it might be hard to figure out why I left. Well, I can sum up the reason in two words: Jim Phillips. Jim Phillips got me to leave Southern Illinois. The opportunity was there to coach Division I football with him at Northern Illinois University, and Jim Phillips is one persuasive guy. I could have stayed at Southern Illinois, just like at Webb City or other places I had been, and been very happy and content forever. But I thought, *You know what? Maybe I should give this a shot.*

SIU had lost a big game to Delaware and future Baltimore Ravens quarterback Joe Flacco, and the very next day I got a call from Jim Phillips. He wanted Rebecca and me to meet him and NIU's former Coach, Joe Novak, at a hotel room in Marion, Illinois. The room was unbelievable. I will never forget it. I mean, this room was decorated top to bottom with Northern Illinois University stuff. I thought for a minute I was already there. They had Northern Illinois University Huskies stuff everywhere!

They were recruiting me, and it wasn't hard to get in the mood very quickly. It was a chance to become a head coach in Division I football and also gave my staff and me a chance to make more money, and that was good. Getting a raise was fine, but what was really important to me was to be able to get a bigger salary for my staff. Believe me, they had earned it.

When we went to SIU, my coaches were not making much money. As far as I was concerned, I was doing pretty well, because I was at about $90,000 a year, a very good salary, but some of my coaches were far from that amount. Some of the other guys were at maybe $40,000 or even as low as $20,000, and that bothered me.

When we arrived at Northern Illinois University, we took over a program that had been struggling. They had a lot of injuries, but we had some tough, hard-nosed players there. Coach Novak, who had been at Northern Illinois before us, had done a good job as head coach. Injuries and losing coaches who went other places had hurt the program.

We went in there and recruited hard. We had some very tough kids, some good players who got us to three straight bowl games. Trevor Olson played offensive tackle for us, and he played in 54 straight football games in his collegiate career. Think about that: 54 straight games! He would play no matter what. I mean, he could break his damn arm or anything else, and he would be out there.

We had good football teams because we had good players—guys like Jordan Lynch, Chandler Harnish, and so many others. I just can't start naming them because I will forget some, and they all deserve mentioning. On that football team, nobody wanted to go and see the trainer for an injury. I would go in that training room, and if I saw anyone in there, I would holler out, "What the hell is going on in here?"

I recall one time there was a group of kids I didn't think were very tough, so I put a bunch of soft-batch cookies in their lockers. They got the point rather quickly. But most of our guys were tough football players, which had a lot to do with the great job of recruiting that we did.

Mike Reis was right when he said better players make better coaches; that was proven out over the years at both Southern and Northern Illinois. But I'm not convinced he thought I was right when I told him maybe a better play-by-play guy would improve the basketball team!

When I got the job at Northern Illinois University, I had the opportunity to meet their legendary former quarterback, George Bork. George once engineered a 60–0 win over Winona State in the early 1960s. After the game a newspaper account read, "George Bork threw touchdown passes at will." His records are almost beyond belief. I had dinner with him, and he is a really good person. I found the donors and other people connected with the program were top shelf all the way as well.

Jim Phillips is at Northwestern now and is one of the finest athletic directors ever to hold the position anywhere. He has proven that by being voted as one of the top people at his position in the country. Jim is just a great person and really knows his role. He knows how to treat people right and spread his vast knowledge, making everyone work harder and become better people.

We were together just a short time at NIU, and I was fortunate for every minute of it. I had been lucky because up to that point in my career, I had been blessed with wonderful athletic directors, and Jim was one of them.

When Jim left, Jeff Compher came in from the University of Washington, and we also had a great relationship. We got the program going and had a solid three years there, and then the University of Minnesota came calling.

My staff and I had been having great success. We had good kids and had kept most of our staff. We picked up a few more coaches and lost a couple but kept the great nucleus of our staff together. Two of our additions who later followed me to Minnesota were Jeff Phelps and Adam Clark, both great additions and super individuals.

I also had P.J. Fleck for a short time before he ended up going to Rutgers. We replaced him with Jimmy Zebrowski, who later came with me to Minnesota. Another coach I want to mention who also came to Minnesota with us was Billy Miller, who did a great job for us and is now at Florida State.

I loved our players at Northern Illinois. They wanted to win in the worst way and played with a chip on their shoulder. We were damn good, too, and won a lot of games, including beating some good Big Ten teams. We went to a bowl game every year with those kids, and they have been winning ever since we left. I am very proud of what my staff and I accomplished at NIU.

In 2010 we lost in the championship game and came home in the middle of the night, and there was snow everywhere. We were pushing cars and trying to get everyone home. It was as bad as it gets. We finally got home and got a little rest. The call from the University of Minnesota came that next morning.

Joel Maturi, the athletic director at Minnesota, and President Bob Bruininks wanted to meet Rebecca and me at the airport in Chicago. I recall getting a call from my agent, Jordan Bazant, and he said, "Hey, they are going to offer you the job at Minnesota. You're the man. You're the builder of programs, and they want you."

So Rebecca and I met Maturi and Bruininks and ended up closing the restaurant at the airport, just the four of us sitting there. They told me everything about the program. I heard about the media and how tough they were, what had happened with the program, and so on. I got an earful of everything. It was another program that had been on the losing cycle for years. Hell, their last trip to the Rose Bowl had been in 1962, and their last Big Ten championship was shared in 1967.

I remember asking them, "How long do I have to make a decision?" And they said, "Well, we would like to know tonight." That wasn't much time, so Rebecca and I walked around some and called my family, talked to my mom and my brother, and really mulled it all over.

I was told I could not say anything to anyone, but I had to talk with my family. To be honest, not one of them wanted me to go to Minnesota. They felt I should stay at Northern Illinois and live happily ever after. But at the same time, they knew me, and this was a chance to go to the Big Ten conference. It was going to be difficult to turn down the offer.

So I took the job at Minnesota. Four of us came to the Twin Cities originally: Tracy Claeys, Matt Limegrover, Rebecca, and I made the trip. Everyone else stayed back to get ready for the bowl game. After the game, the rest of my staff joined me, except for Tom Matukewicz, who stayed and became NIU's defensive coordinator.

This move was not a big problem for our girls because they were older and out of high school. When we went to Northern Illinois, my daughter Tasha was going to be a senior in high school, and she didn't want to go. She wanted to finish her last year of high school. We were just fortunate that we were friends with a family, the Krones, who let Tasha stay with them for her last year. They were great Christian people who really helped us out. It worked out well, and Rebecca went back and forth to spend time with Tasha. So this change was easier in that regard, anyway.

One of the things that really sold me on Minnesota was Joel Maturi. I have great respect for Joel. He is a soft-spoken and very kind man. Jim Phillips had told me a lot about Joel and what a good guy he is. I think in many ways, it was Jim Phillips who at the end of the day got me the job at Minnesota. In fact, I'm sure of it.

I know Jim and Joel had a good relationship, and they had a mutual trust for each other. The fact is, Joel rolled the dice on me. I don't think there was a person in the Twin Cities who thought I could coach anything, let alone in the Big Ten conference. Hell, most of the Minnesota people had never heard of Coach Kill from Northern Illinois. Although I will say we had gone up there with our Northern Illinois football team and beaten the Gophers the year before.

Joel is as good a guy as you will ever meet. He did so much for us, even offering us the use of his home at one point. His wife, Lois, is the same; you can't meet better people than those two. I will always be grateful to them, and they mean the world to me. I feel from the bottom of my heart that everything I have today at this point in my life I owe to Joel Maturi. I am so very thankful that he came into my life as a professional and as a person. I enjoyed every moment I was with him.

When I arrived in Minnesota, it was very difficult. No one knew much about me, and there were all kinds of rumors of coaches who had turned down the job. I had very little sleep and was going to have a press conference right away. There were a bunch of coaches at Minnesota who weren't sure what was going to happen to them, and I'm sure a lot of media and others were wondering, *Why in the hell did they hire this guy?*

This was not the ideal setting to walk into. I don't blame them. There had been talk about some big names going to U of M. People had been excited and disappointed, and then here I come. Most people didn't have a clue who I was and what I was going to do. Believe me, I know there was a lot of, "Jerry *who?*"

I found out one thing right away: there was great worry about the Twin Cities media. I was being told all the points I needed to touch on for the press conference. I had all kinds of advice and counsel from the sports media people at the university as to what to say and what not to say. I can recall saying to them, "No offense, but I don't need anyone to write out for me what I am going to say. If what I tell them at the press conference isn't good enough for them, then I don't really care."

In actuality, I think the press conference went pretty well, and it was kind of an introduction for the media as to who I was and what I stood for. I just talked from my heart, as I have done all my life.

And then we went to work. We had a mess in front of us. We had four kids who were ready to be kicked out of school. We had 21 kids on academic probation, and we faced losing points on our APR (academic progress rating), which would have hurt us on scholarships. We had a lot of work to do, and that wasn't even on the football field!

We started chipping away and working on everything. One of the real down times was telling all the other coaches they were not going to be retained. The only person I kept around the football program was Dan O'Brien, and I will say this: Dan O'Brien is the best hire I ever made. And when I got Adam Clark, who had been with me at Northern Illinois, and Dan together running the football operations part, I called them the Dynamic Duo!

Dan was a good guy and had been with the program for a while and knew what was going on. Joel had told me about Dan, and it wasn't long before I knew I needed him. The first two or three days, he told me everything. He told me where I should go, whom I should meet. And I thought early on, *Man, I have to keep this guy here with me. He knows everybody and is well respected.* Over time, we became very close and I really counted on Dan. And Adam was the same way. He was a tremendous help to me in every way possible. Two great guys who have done more for me than they will ever know!

Most of my staff from Northern Illinois came with me, and they knew how to do what we needed to do. Most of us had been together for quite some time and knew how to turn programs around.

Things were not good with the program. But I never knew the academics were as bad as they were. I didn't know the weight room was that bad. I certainly didn't know the indoor facility was that bad. Still, it wasn't like we hadn't seen things like that before. So we knew what to do and we started to do it immediately.

We rebuilt the program. It didn't matter if it was the business side of it or football, it all had to be done. We set our vision and began to work on it. We didn't do it on our own. We had a lot of help from a lot of people. In some respects, we had better facilities at Northern Illinois than what we started with at Minnesota. Our academics staff did a tremendous job, and Regent Larson came through for us with his support. They just believed in me, and I have never forgotten it.

I met with the team and told them what we were going to do. I told them if they wanted to win, then they had to follow our plan. We were not going to deviate from it, because it had worked in the past and it was going to work at Minnesota. But it wasn't easy. We had to change the culture at the school and, for that matter, within the whole state and how it looked at Gophers football. There were a lot of culture changes made.

We knew we had brought in a good coaching staff, so we didn't have to start from scratch. We worked to get better players, better equipment, a better weight room, a better academics program, and so many other things. But this wasn't trial and error or experimentation; this was what we had done in the past. We knew it would take time but it would work.

With all these things coming, it built on our philosophy that if a player feels good and looks good, he will play good. And we had proven that out everywhere we had been.

It took a while. When we got there, we didn't have players recruited by us. That came the second year. What we wanted took time for the players to understand. It wasn't their fault. This was all new to them. Some bought in right away and some didn't.

I knew we would have to improve our weight program and our weight-lifting facilities. I knew we could do that with Eric Klein, who I think is the best strength coach in the business. We had to increase our weight room staff, and we did. I knew we needed to improve so many other things too, like the indoor facility.

How could we bring players into a program at Minnesota when we had to compete with places like Nebraska, Michigan, and Ohio State? We didn't have a chance! We had to go out and find the right players for us, and we did.

Our first year, Gary Tinsley, one of our players, died in the dormitory. I had gotten to know him that first year. He was a great kid. I arranged for the whole team to travel to Jacksonville, Florida, for the funeral and to support the family. Gary kind of brought us all together in his own tragic but unique way.

We did some personal things for the family, and the administration stepped up and made the travel happen, which was very important to the family and to our football program. And most of all, it was the right thing to do. And to this day, the celebration of this young man remains. He has a presence in the locker room and the team takes a knee for Gary Tinsley before every practice and every game. It has been pretty special.

Minnesota was very difficult to turn around but was still probably second to what we had to do at Southern Illinois. Minnesota was tough in different ways, though, but through the assistance of others—the great coaches and great kids—the turn was made. We had so many changes to make, and without the support we received, it never would have happened. Changing the culture does not happen overnight. But we never lost our direction. We just kept grinding.

For the players, it was simple. We just told them, "If you do what we want, we will win."

Minnesota was my last stop, and I want to mention something here that has always been very important to me. I say this because it happened so often in my coaching career. It is important not to forget about the significance of leaving a football program for another school. This is especially true when you have turned programs around like my staff and I had at Pittsburg State, Webb City, Saginaw Valley, Southern Illinois, and Northern Illinois. Minnesota was the same, but my leaving there was for other reasons.

I left out Emporia State because it was not quite the same; I had been there only two years. In some of the places I left, I had donors come up with more money to keep me, and I have had others that would get mad and then later say, "Now stay in touch with us, will you?" So it was different everywhere, but I always wanted to be sure I was honest with everyone. I wanted to tell people I was leaving before they found out from other sources, but it's hard with social media and all that.

It is hard for me to remember what happened at each stop along my coaching journey, but I do know there were a lot of things that were very troublesome for me personally. At Saginaw Valley State, for example, I think for the most part they understood because of what was happening to my dad. But I still had people mad at me there. If you are leaving a place and people are mad at you because they want you to stay, then you must have done a good job. If they are happy you are leaving, I would have to guess you must not have done a good job.

It was difficult when I left Emporia State, but nothing at all like later on when I left Southern Illinois. Leaving there was very difficult. My relationships there were incredible. I mean, that's why we built our lake home in the area, because we thought we would be staying for the rest of our lives.

I had taken the football program a long way and really rallied the program, the team, and the community to a winning mentality. It was bad enough to leave, but to go to Northern Illinois...

well...nobody wanted me to do that. People who were there who understood the business were fine with it because they could see the opportunity I had. But the tough thing was it all occurred during Christmas break, so it was hard to let them all know at the same time, even though I did my best to find a way to reach out to them all. I felt bad about that.

What bothers me the most is how hard it is on the players. When I left Northern Illinois to go to Minnesota, it was not good. We had the championship game, and then I took the job at Minnesota two days later and had planned to tell the kids at the football banquet, but social media at Minnesota leaked out the information, and ESPN picked it up and said I was leaving.

Today all the kids have cell phones, and many saw it there, and others saw it on TV. Most heard I was leaving before I even got to them about it. Rebecca and I met with them to tell them, and it was not good. But kids are resilient and forgiving, and for the most part I've maintained relationships with those players. We even got our trip to the Orange Bowl paid for by the school administration.

When we left for Minnesota, I was not feeling good about what had happened. It was really tough. Those were very difficult times for us, but we got through them and kept our great memories of all the wonderful years intact. And then it was on to the University of Minnesota and the Big Ten conference, where our fiercest opponents would be Ohio State, Iowa, Wisconsin, Michigan, Nebraska, and Michigan State, along with a host of other top programs. New challenges came with every move, and this was one of them.

Leaving was always tough, but came with the territory. The changes, leaving people behind, the whole process...it was all hard. I have valued the friendships and the great relationships I have made along the way. And to all those wonderful people I have worked with and had contact with, I deeply thank you and appreciate every one of you!

| four |

Great Places and Great People

WHEN I WENT OFF TO school at Southwestern College in Winfield, Kansas, it really represented my first home away from home. It was a great community. It will always have such a special place in my heart because it is where Rebecca and I got together, got married, and started out on our journey together.

Winfield is a town of a little more than 12,000 people, and the two of us went to a small school so we were able to connect with the community and make a lot of friends. I mentioned before how we both worked at Wheeler's IGA. Rebecca was the best-looking girl who ever worked a cash register, and that might be the most intelligent statement I have ever made. She was and still is a beautiful person. We both worked hard at various jobs, went to school, but still had a lot of fun together. Winfield was like many of the small Minnesota communities, with a college atmosphere kind of like the one at Carleton College in Northfield, Minnesota. We loved it there, and best of all, we found each other there.

As we journeyed through life together, we definitely had some great places we lived on all my coaching stops. Midwest City, Oklahoma, was one of them, and really got me introduced to high school football in Oklahoma. Rebecca and I lived in an apartment complex, and it was nice. We were about 180 miles from our home in Cheney, so it was definitely a ways away, but we adjusted pretty well. As I mentioned, we were only there a short time before heading to Pittsburg State, but the memories are unforgettable.

I got my indoctrination into high school football in Oklahoma when we played Dell City in front of 20,000 fans. I mean, 20,000 people at the game! Let me tell you, it doesn't get any better than that. Our coach was Dick Evans, and Dell City had Henry Manning. They called him "King" Henry, and he was some kind of legend in Oklahoma high school football. I don't know a great deal about him, but I know he won a lot of football games at Dell City.

The game was set in just an awesome venue, and with that kind of a rivalry and such massive attendance at the game, it gives you a good idea of what football meant to the people in that area of the country. This was big-time high school football, and I loved it.

There was great high school football all around Oklahoma, and of course the tone is set by the University of Oklahoma's Sooners in Norman. Midwest City is only 18 miles from Norman, so there was a lot of football around where we lived. I can remember going down there and watching practice, and how special that was. Football is big time and very important in Oklahoma, and we got a real taste of it.

The Sooners, as I mentioned before, had Barry Switzer as their head coach back then, and he was legendary. I can remember him coming to our school and recruiting some of our kids, so I was really into all of it.

Our next stop was Pittsburg, Kansas, when I was hired by Coach Franchione to coach the defense at Pittsburg State. Pittsburg is in southeast Kansas. The community is full of hard-nosed, tough people. There is more money in that area than you would think, and it is filled with great community people. Football is very important there.

Gene Bicknell, one of the big-time owners of Pizza Hut, had a great community influence as well, as did several other company owners. The community is made up of several businesses, many of which are very successful.

The population of Pittsburg is about 20,000, and many of those people surround their lives with Pittsburg State Gorillas football. There are also a lot of small communities around Pittsburg, such as Frontenac, Kansas, where Adam Clark is from. Adam was on my staff at Northern Illinois and Minnesota, and he is a great young man. He was about seven years old playing baseball when I first met him. His daddy and I were on the staff together at Pittsburg State.

It is a great town. When we won the national championship, everyone in the town was having a good time. I mean *everybody*. They love their football there. We loved the community, the area, and the people. It was a great place to live.

Our oldest daughter, Krystal, was born in Pittsburg, Kansas. And there is a famous chicken and steak place called the Idle Hour, and it is the best chicken in the country. We still get it shipped to us from time to time. What a great place to eat. I miss it! I recall when Krystal was born, our friend Doug Barto delivered us a bucket at the hospital.

Pittsburg is typical Kansas—flat and full of great people. It sits right in the corner bordering Missouri and Oklahoma. The Oklahoma line is maybe 30 minutes away, and the Missouri line is maybe 15 minutes away, so we sat right near both states. We did really well recruiting in both those states and for the most part got the kids we wanted.

Next up for us was the opportunity for me to be head coach at Webb City, Missouri, about 35 to 40 minutes from Pittsburg, Kansas. It is a great place, and we were there for two years. It really fit us. It was a blue-collar community with hard-nosed kids, and they really rallied around football and we got it going.

The games were huge at Webb City. People would show up in the mornings with their blankets and put them on the seats to be sure they got a good spot for the game that night. It was unbelievable how they loved their football at Webb City, and they sure did like to win. It is just a small community, and we turned that program into a football powerhouse. We won the first state championship, and that foundation has since led to another 12 titles.

Webb City is right near Joplin, Missouri, where the disastrous tornado hit in 2011. Tasha was born there, so both Webb City and Pittsburg are especially close to our hearts—our kids' hometowns!

People to this day still remember us in Webb City, and when we show up there, we are treated like we are still living in the community and still coaching. You would never know we have been gone for more than 25 years. We have been able to maintain the connection and relationships there and everywhere we have been. When you form friendships like we have, how can you ever let them go?

Our next stop for head coaching was at Saginaw, Michigan. We loved it there. Saginaw is right on the bay; it is just unreal. There are so many things to do there. There is a little German town called Frankenmuth near Saginaw. Bronner's Christmas Wonderland in Frankenmuth is the self-proclaimed largest Christmas store in the world. It is an unbelievable place. All around where we lived are a number of really nice small communities, and we sure did enjoy them.

The football team was sponsored by Hooters—I think the only Division II team in America with that sponsor—and then we had Outback Steakhouse connect with us, and I don't think we ever paid for a meal there. They took great care of us and all our staff. And then when we went to two-a-day practices, we had wings delivered to us from Hooters. I remember I used to think, *I doubt there is a team in the country that has this good a gig.*

We loved our time there, and in addition to having a great team and support throughout the community, it was just a great place to live and raise our kids. We lived in a great neighborhood, and our kids could walk to school some of the time. The winters were not always the best. It was a lot like Minnesota in that regard: cold, windy, and gloomy part of the time, but that was okay, because the rest of the seasons made up for the bad weather. It is a beautiful state.

We ran various camps all over the state and had a great time wherever we were. I can tell a great story about that too. We ran an Option Football Camp in Lowell, Michigan, and several of us were staying at the lake house belonging to Noel Dean, the football coach at Lowell High School. I was standing on a Jet Ski talking to some guys, and Tracy Claeys was skiing on one and coming in toward the dock. Well, he figured his distance wrong and came in way too fast and hit me full blast and knocked me about eight feet in the air. I thought I was dead! I really did. Tracy is a big guy, and when he hit me, I thought my life was over. They still tell that story about Tracy almost killing me.

Coach Rob Reeves had played for me in the past and now coached with me, and his wife, Angie, played basketball there and worked for me. So Angie and I would go to the basketball court and take on Coach Reeves and Coach Klein and go to war. And there was one thing I learned during those spirited games: Angie was a lot tougher than Rob! I was glad she was on my team!

Our time in Saginaw was fantastic, but Emporia, Kansas, was next, as we wanted to be closer to my mom and dad. It turned out to be another great community. It is a hilly area that sits right in the middle between Kansas City and Wichita. The town is about 25,000 people, and there is a meat-packing plant there. There were a lot of country folk around with cattle and that kind of thing. It was a real quaint kind of town, and they loved their football! It was the place I mentioned earlier where we built one of the new facilities in about four months.

It was a fun time for us. I had a young woman who worked with me there named Melissa Haab, a southern girl who was instrumental in helping us get kids we recruited into school. She was our admissions director, and if we needed to get a kid in school, she would pull out all the stops to help out.

The people in the community were really down to earth and would do anything to help you out. My kids loved it there. Krystal was able to play on a softball team, and she was a good player, and Tasha was playing basketball and going to camps. Emporia was a good basketball school and something Tasha loved, but we had to move again, this time to Southern Illinois University. And it was tough; no question about that.

I talked earlier about the beginning of our ride coaching at Southern Illinois, and although we loved the new location, it was not easy to move on. It took about six months after I left with the coaches before our families were able to join us, so we had that lapse of time together again, but we made it work.

I loved the Southern Illinois community, the whole Carbondale area. Tremendous people live there. We have made so many great lifelong friends; it is just such a special area for us. Tasha got married there last year, and Joel Maturi and so many others from all over came to the wedding. It is great country, with great people, and it likely will be our permanent home someday.

We were a perfect fit for Southern Illinois. It was blue jeans country, and that's what appealed to me. The football program began to take off, we got our facilities built, and for a 1AA school, it became one of the top facilities in the country. We could not have been more proud of what that football program accomplished, and yet the friendships we made have been as important to us.

I have as good a friend as you can have there by the name of Brent Gentry, who is a county commissioner, and to this day if I call him and say "Hey, I'm coming to town," he will have a boat all ready for me to get some fishing in. Those kinds of people are all throughout the area.

Once we had a fishing tournament to raise money for the school, and pretty much everyone showed up. There was a monster fish fry that almost everyone joined in on. I visited a little place called Mary Lou's often, and still do. It is the kind of place you can go in and bring four people, and all the meals together might cost 20 bucks. Southern Illinois is a neat place, and has a little different cost of living too.

When we went to Northern Illinois, obviously things were different. It was maybe the first time we really felt like we had left our home, because we were so fond of Southern Illinois in Carbondale.

Northern Illinois University is located in DeKalb, Illinois, home of the cornfields and the wind, baby! It is about an hour from Chicago, and the wind blows like you have never seen it before. And it is cold as hell there, just like in Minnesota. It is flat and full of cornfields. It's like they went out in a cornfield and put a school there.

It is a great area, with wonderful people, and we loved it there! I would be very remiss if I didn't just say one word about our time at Northern Illinois: Fatty's. They have the best pretzel bites, and I mean the best in the entire world! And outside this great eating place there was a sign that read COACH KILL PARKING. I mean I had my own place to park outside Fatty's. Hell, there was a time I didn't even have that at the University of Minnesota.

The only regret was that we only had three years there, which was not enough time. I guess I could say that about every place we lived. It was never long enough.

There is no doubt I am a country boy, but I also loved the Twin Cities when we arrived to coach at the University of Minnesota. I truly loved the Twin Cities. We had an opportunity to do so many things and meet so many great people. Everyone was so good to us. We have tried to give back to the community because it treated us so well.

We received anything we ever needed. We made so many great relationships that we will never forget. We are so thankful for everything and the many friendships we made.

As I move toward closure in this chapter, all I can say is a heartfelt appreciation for being so blessed to have met and enjoyed so many great people and so many great places in all our football stops. It has been a wonderful and inspirational journey to this point. As for the future, I'm sure whatever it holds will be as exciting and meaningful.

We have had some wonderful opportunities to move around the Midwest. We have lived in tremendous communities and met great people. Each place we have been had its own special qualities, so we have always felt blessed to be in a profession that has given us such opportunity.

However, all the moving, all the long workdays and late hours, and my inability to leave work at work has taken its toll, especially in the beginning of our marriage, and I would be remiss not to mention it here.

We were married very young. Rebecca was only 19 and I was 21. When we went to Midwest City, she was still finishing her schooling. I'm not sure her family was all fired up about us getting married at such a young age. My family was fine with it because they knew Rebecca was such a great person. She had promised her dad she would finish her education, and I made the same promise to him. She had to go about it the long way, and here I was having a great time coaching at Midwest City. It didn't seem quite fair.

I was living the dream. We would go to the Oklahoma football games on Saturday, and Rebecca never got to go with us because she was working and doing her job to help us out, and then also going to school. I know it was not a great experience for her.

When we moved to Pittsburg State, I was working for Coach Franchione, and we would be at work from daybreak to late in the evenings. It would be maybe 10:00 or 11:00 at night—or sometimes even 1:00 or 2:00 in the morning—before I would get home. It was definitely the life of a football coach, but it didn't do much for our time together and our marriage.

Age three: many years ago, my mother captioned this "our little angel."

Posing in my Little League uniform at age nine.

Christmas 1962. That's me in the front with Dad, Mom, and my little brother, Frank.

Dad and Mom are the most important influences of my life.

A glimpse into my long-haired, football playing days.

Rebecca and me on our wedding day, with her parents.

Celebrating my first coaching success, with the 1989 state champion Webb City High School football team.

With the coaching staff at Pittsburg State—an incredible group of guys. Dennis Franchione (back row, fourth from left), whom I played for, gave me my first job as a college coach.

Walking the sideline with Krystal at Saginaw Valley State University.

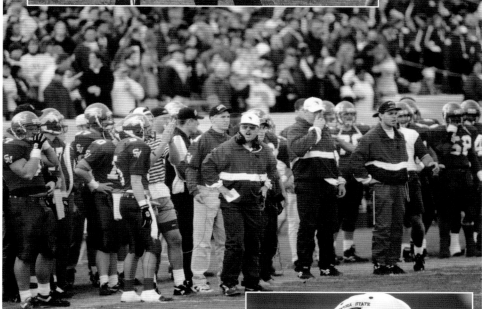

Coaching the Cardinals in November 1994.

New school, new look: clean-shaven during my first year at Emporia State in 1999.

Tasting success at Southern Illinois.

Arguing the Salukis' to the head linesman.

Rebecca and I were also proud to contribute to the greater community while at SIU. We established the Coach Kill Fund to contribute to cancer victims. Robert Holley (seated, center) is one of the many people the foundation has helped. We marched the field at halftime to raise money and awareness for "Tackling the Tough Times" and beating cancer.

Honoring Robert Holley was a privilege for us and the Salukis family.

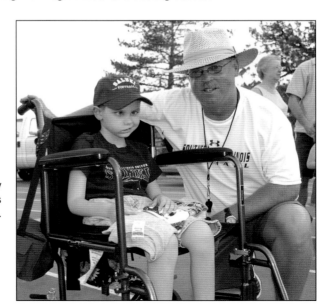

Rallying the team at Northern Illinois.

I am pretty sure during these times, Rebecca must have thought, *What the hell have I gotten myself into? This is absolutely crazy!* And then on weekends, you know, I would be around Coach Fran talking football, playing golf, that kind of thing, which basically kept me away from home all the time. Coach Fran was another guy who worked hard, and I wanted to be around him, to find ways to impress him.

I recall one night while I was doing all this, I came home and Rebecca told me she needed to leave and go back home. I asked her what she meant, and she said, "I need to leave and go back home and figure this all out. I am really struggling with this. And I just don't know." There were some other things involved, and she was not sure about it all. So she left me for about a week and a half and went back home.

It was a very difficult time for both of us. I remember calling my dad and saying, "Dad, this ain't good. I love this girl and I have never lost at anything in my life, and I don't want to start now." He said to me, "Well, you better figure this out, and you better get her back there. You are going to have to make some changes in the way you are doing things."

I can recall saying to him, "I don't know how to do that and still keep everybody happy." I was really confused. Dad said, "Well, you are going to have to try to keep everyone happy if you want her back."

Rebecca came back shortly after, and we went to see a priest. As I look back on it, it was interesting, because the priest spent very little time talking to Rebecca. He spent almost the whole time talking to me. I guess he felt I needed the counseling the most, and he was right! There was no doubt about that. He told me about all my flaws—and let me tell you, there were many! And he never really said anything to Rebecca about anything.

I made a commitment that I would try to do my best, and our marriage grew just like my knowledge grew about coaching football. I had to learn how to be married. Fortunately we were very young, and we both grew with it. Rebecca was able to finish school, and she actually graduated from Southwestern College because they allowed her to transfer credits.

I had to learn what was going on from her perspective; I had to see it from her side. At the time, I had no clue what was going on with us. As I said, I was living the dream, but it sure wasn't her dream. I finally got it and eventually found a way to make it work for both of us. I worked with her, and she worked with me.

Marriage is the toughest thing you will ever do in life. I truly believe that. It is so easy to go get a divorce, give up on the conflicts, and never give the marriage a chance. People are going to have difficulties. There are going to be things in life that are not perfect.

Over the years, there is no question in my mind I have learned as much about marriage as I have learned about football. It is such an important part of my and Rebecca's life. I know our marriage has grown stronger through the adversity and years together. The longer we have been married, the better it has become.

We are blessed with two beautiful girls who are the best. Over the years of our marriage, Rebecca became a part of my life, and I became a part of hers. She joined me and I joined her, and our kids did the same.

The football teams became a part of all our lives too, and it made our lives together so very special. As the head football coach, I wanted our family to be part of the team as if we were doing it all together. And we did, and it was the greatest.

Moving to new places was always difficult, but what we developed family-wise, friendship-wise, and experience-wise will bless us forever.

| five |

The Kill Way

COACHING FOOTBALL HAS BEEN a dream come true that I have lived for more than three decades. It has been a great career, and I have been proud of the accomplishments of our teams over the years. There is no question that any kind of success comes from a variety of people working hard and doing their jobs. I do believe, however, that success does not come about by accident but by having a strategic plan and a philosophy in place.

I believe I left every program I have been at in better shape than it was in when I arrived. I am not taking the credit for that but spreading it out to all my staff who have worked to make that happen.

I'm not sure most fans really know what goes into coaching a football team. It's far more than having a few practices during the week and then running out on the field on Saturday afternoons. Our teams have had success and we have been able to turn programs around because of many dedicated people following a philosophical plan that has evolved over the years.

Recruiting

Recruiting is the lifeblood of any program, because if you don't have good players and players that fit into what you want to accomplish, you have no chance to win. I have been in unusual situations in my coaching stops. I have never been involved with the Ohio States, Texases, or USC programs, where they have everything you could ever want to show off to potential players. I have coached in many places that didn't have the facilities to compete on an even playing field.

Basically everywhere I have coached, we built facilities. And I never had the opportunity to be in any of them, because I had moved on by the time they were done and ready for occupancy. And yet I have been proud of what we put in place for the next group of coaches, players, and fans.

The number one thing with recruiting is to first talk about academics. Kids' families want to hear about the education their children are going to receive if they come to our school. They want to know what the school has to offer from the educational standpoint.

For example, being at the University of Minnesota, my last stop, we certainly couldn't recruit based on how good the football team was at that time, but we could recruit on the institution and the great reputation the university has in many different areas. We could focus on the business program and how strong that program is, the education programs, the medical school and how they fit into the community with such things as internships.

With regard to the business part, we could talk about all the Fortune 500 companies and how those opportunities would be there for young men after graduation. We would spend time talking about the educational advantages of coming to play football at Minnesota.

We would carefully look at the academic background of the kids we were recruiting, but we have found that *wanting to* go to school and *wanting to* play can be every bit as important as a good-looking high school academic record. I have been given a gift in recruiting in that I have the ability to get a good feel about a potential recruit having that want-to attitude.

We certainly talk with the kids and their parents about the academics, but we also find that some kids just want to play and don't have an initial interest in all the other stuff. But I promise you, the parents in most situations are very interested in the academic side of it.

I tell the recruits straight out that the rules regarding an education are very simple: if you don't go to class, you don't play. I want them to know right up front how important it is for them to go to class and graduate. The families will almost always jump on board with that. But it is not just a selling pitch for the parents. It's bred into our philosophy to graduate all of our players.

Another major thing I do with each kid is to say to them, "Hey, do you love football? Do you really love the game?" And then I will go over the schedule with them and what we do on a day-to-day basis, and then I ask them again about loving the game. "Do you love the game? I mean, really now, do you love the game of football? Because you have to love the game to be successful."

I bet I say that four or five times over the course of time I am visiting with them. I want to get a feel for their love of the game. It's important because it shows on the field and in the classroom, and I want them to understand they have to go to class and do well if they want to play. So the bottom line is if they love football that much, they will also understand the only way to exercise that love is to attend class and do well.

You want to get to know the kids you are recruiting. And you want to get to know their families through the process that you have, and you don't have a lot of time to do that. As the head coach, I am allowed to get into the home only one time, so I really have to do a good job when I make the visit.

When you get into a house, you really get a chance to see a young man and how he fits in and what he is about, because you see kids from all different cultures, all different backgrounds, and from all different areas of the country. You have got to be able to relate to all kinds of different people. And through this process it helps you to get to know the young men and how you are going to coach them.

When we first look to recruit kids, the first things we look at from an athletic standpoint are length and speed. How tall are they? How long are their arms and legs? How fast are they? I had a strength coach, Eric Klein, who was with me for 21 years, and I counted on him a lot to tell me about a kid we might be recruiting. We wanted a kid who could run, and most of the time we were not going to recruit a kid who did not have good speed and good height. Sometimes we would go after a young man who was shorter than what we generally wanted, but most of the time length was critical, because we always figured we could put the weight on him. So speed and body length are very important.

As far as personality, sometimes we could be fooled, but we wanted real quality guys. This is when you go into the schools and find out about the person. How do they get along with other kids? How hard do they work? Do they play with enthusiasm? Are they on time for things?

And then you go to the games. If they play basketball, you go watch them. If they play football, you go to the practices and the games. You are looking for kids who play hard all the time, and I mean *all* the time. We definitely would not recruit a kid who did not play hard all the time. We watched them. There is nothing better than the eyeball as far as telling you about a recruit. We watched film on the young men, looked at their academic records, and basically found out everything we could about them as athletes and as people.

One of the very first things I said to kids when I was at U of M and made that first contact was to mention the great Twin

Cities area and the school, because they had never seen it. At Southern Illinois, I would say something like, "Southern Illinois is a great place to live and go to school. It is a beautiful setting and a great campus." And then I would talk about the community surroundings, the great school, and the football program, and how it was moving in the right direction. I would say something about how much we needed them in our program and that we felt they were a great fit for us.

Recruiting is as important as just about anything you do, and to be successful you have to find the right kids for your program. We give it as much attention as anything, because without the right players, you will never have a chance to win.

Facilities

When it comes to the facilities on campus, the first and most important thing to evaluate is the academic facilities. If your players are not eligible academic-wise, they can't play. So when I go into a place, I look at academics first. Do we have enough tutors? How many computers do we have? How many academic advisors do we have to help the kids? That is exactly what we did at the University of Minnesota, Northern Illinois, Southern Illinois, and every other stop we have made.

And then the next thing you have to take a look at is the weight room. Going back to Minnesota, when we arrived, they had two strength coaches and everyone else in the Big Ten had five. So we had to get that number increased to five, and then we had to take a look at the weight room. We needed improvement in that area as well.

Every place we went, the weight room was a problem. And there was never any money available for improvement. I always teased Paul Kowalczyk when he was the athletic director at Southern Illinois that he deliberately couldn't find the light switch for the weight room because he didn't want me to see how bad it was. And as I said, it was bad! I mean, we lifted in a weight room that was smaller than what we had at the high school in Webb City.

So about all you can do in the beginning is put a fresh coat of paint on it, try to get some extra equipment, and do the best you can until there are funds to get it done right. You have to take what you have and make it the very best you can. What other choice do you have?

We always operated under the belief that you cannot complain internally about what you don't have; your job is to do that to the administration. With the players we tried to sell a poor weight room as unique and tell them that at some point we would have new facilities because we had been able to improve them everywhere previously.

The weight room is essential, because that's the place where you get the players bigger, stronger, and faster, and if you are unable to do that because of the space or the equipment, then you are not going to win. And then academically, if the players are not doing what they are supposed to be doing, they can't play. So those are two of the facilities you want to focus on. Academics and the weight room are critical if you want to have any kind of success.

The third thing you want to focus on is where you are going to practice. I call those areas our operating facilities, because that's where the kids are going to be working all the time. Where is this going to be? Do we have two practice fields and enough space to get our work done?

We know that we are likely going to play some of our games on grass and some games on artificial turf. So do we have a grass field? Do we have a turf field? How much room do we have? Do we have two fields side by side? This makes the transition to drill work faster. How much equipment do we have? Do we have a two-man sled and a seven-man sled?

This is all important, and we need these kinds of things. I have been places where we built our own stuff! If we had to have a particular thing to give us a better chance to become successful, and we didn't have the money, we just built it ourselves.

Where do the players eat, and what kind of nutrition program do they have? Players have to feel good about where they are, whether it be at meals, at the players' lounge, or wherever else it might be.

Having said all this, can you imagine the difficulty in recruiting kids where you are basically starting from scratch with the weight room, practice areas, and places to eat, and you have to compete with Ohio State, Michigan, USC, and so on for the best kids? I mean, it was virtually impossible. That's why all those things are so important to a successful program. It is so basic. When kids now walk in, they want the "wow factor." And the problem was that our competition for kids often had the wow factor, and we didn't.

You may have a brand-new stadium, but the kids may only get over to the stadium 10 or 12 times a year and that's it, unless you are practicing at the stadium on a regular basis. Don't get me wrong; the stadium is important, because kids will be more impressed the nicer it is, but all the other things, such as the weight room and dining facilities, are just as important if not more so.

At Northern Illinois we had no practice facility, so we had to practice at the stadium. We even had to clear snow off the field from time to time. Hell, I've shoveled snow off the field right alongside some of the kids who were doing a little disciplinary punishment. We had to do it in order to practice.

At Southern Illinois we had the worst stadium in college football, maybe in the *history* of college football. At least that's the way I felt when I first saw it. I will say this though: we did have good practice facilities at Southern Illinois. They were grass, and the fields were side by side, so it was great for getting our work done. We stayed off the stadium field as much as possible because I always called it the worst turf in college football at the time.

Despite what I said about the facilities, our academics at SIU were near the top of the charts when it came to graduating African Americans. We were in the top four in the nation in this regard, so that was pretty special for us. We tried always to look for those things that were unique to everyone else, and to use them to assist in our recruiting.

Coaching Staff

When I look at assembling a coaching staff, the first thing I do is try to find the right fit for each position. But the most important part of finding the right coach is also finding someone who knows how to work. I don't care what division they come from, what conference they have been in, or any of that stuff. What I care about is, do they know how to work?

I was raised with an unbelievable work ethic from my dad, and it was strengthened by coaching under Coach Franchione, so I know all about working. I do a significant amount of checking on a coach's background and find out all about him. Is he a grinder? Does he want to win? What is his attitude on working hard? All of these kinds of things come first when trying to find someone to work for, and with, me. Experience and knowledge of all areas of the game aren't that important, because I can teach them those things. I want to know if they know how to work.

The other thing that works for me is that by the time I became a head coach, I had developed a coaching tree. I had a list of a lot of guys I had worked with and whom I knew well. I would bring in a lot of graduate assistants, guys who had coached in high school, guys with good reputations, and so on.

Tracy Claeys, now the University of Minnesota head coach, came to work for me for about $600 a month. He was highly recommended. And he was with me a long time, some 20-plus years. We didn't have the money to pay much, so it was easy to find those who were committed to the game and knew how to work.

Tracy was a really quiet guy. He was a math major, very smart, and he could handle the budget part of it. And the plus with Tracy was also that he was a good football coach. He knew how to work. He has the commitment and great work ethic, so we were a great fit for two decades.

I brought Jay Sawvel with me. My high school coach knew Jay from back at Notre Dame camps. I also knew people at Notre Dame who said, "This guy is terrific. He is going to be a great recruiter and has a great mind for the game." Jay was a secondary coach and we needed someone like him when we hired him. He fit our need in the secondary, had a great background, had good recommendations, and knew how to work. He was perfect.

As far as the quarterbacks coach, I always wanted a guy who was going to be able to relate to my quarterbacks. I usually wanted a guy who had played the position and was smart. In fact, all my staff had to be smart and know the game of football. Ideally if you can find someone who has the work ethic and the experience in several facets of the game, you are on the right track in the hiring process.

My thinking was if I could find some who had played the game and had great passion for the game and worked hard, I likely had the right person. And if I found this person and he lacked some in experience for certain parts of the game, as I said, I could teach him.

I have spent a lot of my time teaching my assistant coaches about parts of the game they may be somewhat unfamiliar with. At the same time, many of the coaches whom I have hired have taught me some things about the games as well. I don't care how much experience someone has, there is always room for more learning. Even after being in the game for more than 30 years, I was always hungry to learn more and become better at what I did.

I mostly hired guys I already knew from various kinds of experiences with them, but on occasion I would hire people I didn't know. In those instances, I did my homework on them from talking to others I knew in the business. I like to think I was smart enough to have figured out what I needed in surrounding myself with people who could make up for my weaknesses.

I wanted coaches who had my work ethic and who were tough individuals. I didn't want any soft football team, and I sure didn't want any soft coaches on my staff. Soft was not acceptable.

I had a reputation of having coaches stay with me for a long time. I had some for 20 years, others for 15, and so on. We developed great relationships over the years and won a lot of football games together. I have been asked, "Why? Why do you have coaches stay with you for so long, some even turning down head coaching jobs to stay on your staff? Why?"

It can be summed up in one word: *loyalty*. I was loyal to them, and they were loyal to me. *Loyalty* is a big word, and you know it doesn't come around very often with people. And so when it does, it is special.

I always tried to look out for my coaches. I worked hard to take care of them financially or to assist them in any way I could. There was good chemistry between all of us, and as we moved from place to place, they certainly enhanced their coaching reputations and their pay.

We all worked hard together, and they knew they would be a part of the decision-making process. I carried the final decision responsibility as the head coach, but my coaches knew they would always have input into what we were going to do.

When we moved on to new environments, I always felt it was necessary to bring my staff with me. Some felt that was not always the best idea, but it worked for me and kept the trust, loyalty, and continuity together. And we were successful in every place we went.

I tried to treat my coaches well, always tried to help them, and worked hard to create a good working atmosphere and environment. I think it was appreciated.

Support Staff

When it comes to support staff, I honestly think I am partial to them. I love them as much as anybody, maybe more! As I look back on secretaries, administrative assistants, and all the other roles, I have had tremendous people working for me. As I mentioned, at Southern Illinois, Sharon Lipe was a great inspiration to me and to our program. We didn't have this position and that position for our team in support. Sharon was it; I mean she was *all* of it.

Also on staff—and great to work with in recruiting and other areas—was Tracy Wiseman, who was a really hard worker and fun to be around. Tracy and Sharon were fantastic people and great workers.

At Northern Illinois, Joyce James and Julie Edwards in my office, well, they were incredible. I have always figured that with what they put up from me, they have earned a one-way ticket to heaven. No doubt about that.

I had Rachel Lee, Maddie Hayes, and Jenna Henry at Minnesota, and they were just wonderful. And there were so many others in the support role in areas such as recruiting, player personnel, football operations, equipment, training, and on and on. And every one of them made such an incredible contribution with little if any recognition. I have had tremendous people in these positions, and they don't get paid very much.

These people are without any doubt the true backbone of any football program. They are the ones who do the everyday work. They deserve more money, never complain, and without them, I don't know how a coach could function.

Take the equipment staff as an example. Without them, how could you set up practice? I have always tried to find a way to show them my appreciation because they have been so important to me. In so many places, they are overworked, underpaid, and underappreciated. I did my best to show them how important they were to our program.

I had some great administrative assistants over the years. I mean these wonderful young women always pointed me in the right direction. They did everything. When it came to computers, the Internet, emails, and all that kind of stuff, they did it all. Sometimes because I didn't want to take care of all that, and sometimes because I didn't know how to do it. Sharon Lipe always used to say, "Keep him away from those computers!" She knew me well. They were all special people, and I can never thank them enough.

It takes so many people to operate a successful football program, and no matter what their job, it is important. The janitor is important. Hell, they have to keep the building clean. We were always giving them sweatshirts and T-shirts, and I tried as often as possible to thank them for their great work. As you go down the chain of command, so to speak, it's the people at the lower end of the chain who sometimes make the most difference.

The training room is also essential. If your team is not healthy, you're not going to win. It's as simple as that. I'm one of the few coaches in the country who hired a female trainer, Kammy Powell. She became my trainer at Northern Illinois, and she is as good as it gets. It didn't make a difference to me if you were a woman or a man, or what your background was, I just wanted someone who loved football, believed in what we were doing, and would work his or her butt off. And Kammy at Northern Illinois did that for us. Her role with the team, and how it helped us win, was immeasurable. And wherever she goes, she brings that incredible work ethic and commitment with her as she did when she came to Minnesota. And I cannot ever forget Dr. Pat Smith, who has been on the Gophers sideline for decades. His work and commitment to medically caring for our players is a true commitment to excellence!

Students

When I got to most programs, there was little connection between the football program and the student body. Once we came and the message got out as to what we were doing—and especially when we started to win—gradually the students got involved. But it wasn't easy. I knew the importance of reaching out to students—getting out on campus, going to student events, showing students I was more than a football coach. And gradually, over time, it worked.

At each school we had to find a way for students to buy into the program. We did a variety of things to involve students, such as buying them pizza, arranging for them to have their own tailgate area near the stadium, and personally handing out tickets. We would do everything we could think of to heighten their interest level in their football team.

We tried to find ways to get them involved, such as the Bleacher Creatures I talked about earlier. We had camps for women. Students need to know they can help make a difference and are important to the cause. We told the students, "We need you. We need you to be an important part of your football team because we can't be successful without you."

A coach does a great deal more to be successful than just coach football. Coaches have to find ways to rally the troops, so to speak, and make people see what they are doing is important. And the only way to do that is to go and see people. For example, I have spoken at fraternities and sororities and gone to events with them.

When you show up to places and do things, the word travels. It's like how you get to know the players on your team—you also have to get to know the students who don't play for you, and make them feel like they are a part of the program, that it's their team.

We would let students know they were important in a lot of small ways. For instance, when I had time with the press, I took every opportunity to compliment the students. When we ran out of the tunnel onto the field, we let the students know we knew they were there with us. It made them feel like they made a difference, and they did! It's like anything else—when they feel a part of something, its special.

I have never once said, "It's Coach Kill's football team." I have always said "It is the state's football team, the students' football team, and the university's football team," because it is. All I am is the guy who got paid to put a good product out on the field that people cared about, so they wanted to come. That's all I was supposed to do. And if I did that, then I had done my job. But it wasn't easy, it took a lot of work—far beyond the X's and O's.

Other Groups—Lettermen's Club, Civic Groups, Etc.

Everywhere I have been, I have found the lettermen, the guys who played there, are frustrated with the program or nonexistent. You have to find a way to get them involved, to make them feel appreciated and to communicate with them. You can have a lot of talk, but it doesn't mean anything unless you can back it up. Lettermen have to know they count and that we will listen to them. We wanted them around—to be at practices, to meet the new players, to have special meetings and breakfast gatherings, those kinds of things. We would get them in the locker room with the players from time to time. It all works.

One thing I am very proud of with our football teams is we backed up what we said we were going to do. If we said we were going to get a group involved, we did. If we said we were going to do something, we did it. If we said we would never do something, then we never did it. Your word is your bond, and people need to know they can count on you.

The importance of communication and being visible cannot be underestimated. They are critically important. When I came to Minnesota, I literally did every single thing I was asked to do. It got to be so much, it was virtually impossible to do it all, but I did every possible thing I could do. It got people involved and let them know they counted and were appreciated.

Every place I have been, I traveled around the area, and even the state, to meet people and get to know them. I went to various clubs, such as Rotary Clubs, and anyplace else people wanted me to be. I mean, I just showed up. If I had to stay around after something and sign autographs, I did that.

One of the ways to help the community feel like it is part of the football program is with some mottos. At Minnesota we said we were going to rebuild the program "Brick by Brick." It was effective, and people felt like they could relate to it. At Northern Illinois it was "Doing It the Hard Way," and at Southern Illinois it was "Hard Hat and Lunch Pail."

We worked with donors and potential donors, and got every possible group involved. My wife, Rebecca, has always been involved. She has been a huge part of it to show people how important they are to our football team. She and I have given our hearts and souls to every community we have ever been in. We loved doing it, and the community loved it. As a result, we generated tremendous support and have made lifelong friends.

And the friends we have gained and the connections from football never stop. Even people we don't know seem to connect with us at times. Just recently, we were out with Rebecca's family and this guy—a high school coach in Colorado—came up to me and said, "Hey, Coach, how are you doing?" And I said, "I'm doing okay." And he said, "You know what? I've been following your career all the time you've been coaching. I respect the way you handle kids and how you handled yourself. And I recognized you, and I just wanted to say hi and thank you for what you have done for football." When something like that happens, it makes it all worthwhile. It really means a lot to me.

Media

The media has been quite different in every place I have been. As I moved from place to place, the media attention has gotten bigger. At Northern Illinois, we were close to Chicago, so that made a big difference in the coverage. And then when I came to Minnesota, there was also an even greater difference with the huge Twin Cities area.

Overall, I would say I have always gotten along well with the media. I always tried to treat them fairly and be honest with them. When I was at Southern Illinois, I can recall being told by some media people, "We just don't win at Southern Illinois, and we never will." Some of those people have now become good friends of mine.

At Northern Illinois I had a good relationship with the local media and the Chicago media as well. I was always straight with them but at the same time protected my players, and they understood that.

When players were not playing very well, we said it was clear the coaches weren't coaching very well. If a certain position player didn't play well, then we said the coach didn't coach enough to help him play well. If we didn't have enough good players, then it was our fault as coaches that we didn't recruit well enough. It was that kind of protection we used for our players, and also, it was a fact. I had no problem with that at all. I never blamed the players. But at the same time, when a player got in trouble, I was right on top of it. We would handle it.

Over the years, I feel I was treated very fairly by the media. I always try to answer questions very thoroughly. The media is smart enough to see through people who are not straightforward and honest. I worked hard to have good media relationships, and my way seemed to work. I always tried to make time for the media and never tried to put up smoke screens or cover up anything. I think they appreciated that aspect of our relationship.

New Head Coach—First Players Meeting

One of the problems that always exists with the first players meeting after coming in as the new head football coach is time. Usually we were involved in so many things as we entered a program it was tough to give that meeting the time it deserved. And yet it is a very important first meeting.

Generally, I went in and introduced myself and talked about my philosophy and what I expected out of players. I told them we had been several other places and had won in every one of them. But I told them we won because we did things a certain way, and that's what we would be doing there too. I advised them, "The culture is going to change here, and some of you will make it and some will not." And I said, "As difficult as some of the changes may be, if you do it our way, we will win." I told them our vision and how it was going to be.

I remember one time a kid walked in to the meeting late, and I said, "This will be the last time you will ever walk into a meeting late. It will never happen again!" So I tried to set the tone right away as to how it was going to work.

For the most part, I usually got a good reaction. You have to remember, when we took over programs, they hadn't been winning and were open to what we had to say. I would say, "If you follow me and my staff, and if you listen, good things are going to happen. And if you don't, you probably won't be here. And for the ones that stay, you will get rewarded." That last sentence is a quote from Coach Novak, who preceded me at Northern Illinois. When I arrived there, I saw it posted in the locker room: THE ONES THAT STAY WILL BE REWARDED. He is a special man, and the quote is very fitting when you go in to turn a program around.

Pregame/Postgame Talk

I spent a lot of time during the week talking to our players about the critical points to winning and losing that week's particular football game. Each team we were going to play was a little different, so the talks would vary in content. I emphasized things like the importance of that week's game, no other. The most important game is the one a team is going to be playing right *now*. I tried to come up with a theme for each game and do what I could to get the team to focus on what was right in front of them.

We always started with the Lord's Prayer before we went out, and repeated it when we came back in. And hopefully we came back in with a win.

After a win, I called all my players up and complimented them on playing hard, and depending on the nature of the win, I was even known to do a little dancing. It was time to celebrate!

After a big loss, I didn't say much. I kept it short and didn't pick out any players who might have had a bad game. I talked with the team and told them we were going to evaluate what happened so it did not happen again. I would say, "We are going to look at the film of the game, and we are going to get better." We lost as a team, and we were going to move ahead as a team.

I always said after a win or a loss, "Now, don't go out tonight and do anything stupid, and let's come in here tomorrow and get ready for the next game." Over the years I was pretty lucky in that regard, with very few problems from the kids because of stupid activity.

Fall and Spring Practices

In the spring we worked on things we wanted to do differently. We experimented and saw how it went. We may have wanted to try some players at different positions, that sort of thing. We would focus on some things we didn't do very well in the past season. We also wanted to figure out who the key players were on our team. The practices were generally very physical, and I wanted to know who was tough and who my leaders were.

We also spent a lot of time on technique. We set goals and concentrated on those things, and when spring was over we hoped to have accomplished those goals.

In the fall, we knew we would only have a couple scrimmages. And it was very important at that time to look at the new freshman players who had come in. So we would split up in different ways to do that. We kept the younger guys together and tried to really form some kind of evaluations on them. We needed them to be up to speed with what we were doing and see who could play right away.

We did get physical in the fall but not to the same extent as in the spring. We didn't want to get kids hurt, and we had to get ready for the first game of the new season. Special teams work also got more attention in the fall as we tried to figure out who would contribute on those teams.

One of the things I often talked about was—again—toughness. To me toughness goes a couple ways: you have to be physically tough and mentally tough. Some kids cannot handle the grind of training camp. They can't handle the toughness of it. They make mental mistakes, they are tired and unfocused, and you can tell. When their backs are against the wall, they stand out one way or the other. We did some drills—goal-line situations, for example—that would help us establish who was physically tough enough to play. We also spent a lot of time on tackling drills. We wanted to evaluate kids one-on-one.

Probably the easiest way to find out about mental and physical toughness is to go down to the training room and ask about the kids. I spent a lot of time talking with our strength coaches. Our staff could tell me who was doing this and that: who could handle the running, the lifting; how the kids performed over the summer; which kids were doing their work. All those things gave us a good handle on the toughness of our kids and our team.

These practices went hand in hand with discipline. Discipline is so important, and it can be summed up quite easily with four simple rules:

1. Be on time.
2. Act right.
3. Go to class.
4. Play like hell on Saturday.

Social Media and the Internet

When you look at the whole thing of social media, there have certainly been a lot of changes, some for the better and some for the worse. You know, from a coaching standpoint, social media is somewhat of a nightmare. That and texting are the ways kids communicate now; they rarely use the telephone.

Through various things like Facebook, kids are always telling everyone else what they are doing. Hell, I don't want people to know what I'm doing, but this is the new way, and all kids are doing it. So we had to actually have someone monitoring all our kids and what they were doing on Facebook, Twitter, and other sites they might be using for communication purposes.

Social media was a huge undertaking for us in recruiting, though. It's amazing what people are willing to share with each other. We had the ability to find out just about anything you would want to know about a young man by this type of monitoring. We had support staff who did all this monitoring for us, and there wasn't much that got by them.

We had four full-time staff and three students who worked on recruiting for us, and by the way, some teams have as many as 10 staff that do nothing but watch and gather information for recruiting.

I'm an old-school guy, so much of this stuff was foreign to me. But I was smart enough to know this was the direction we were headed in and that it was a must in our operation in order to be successful. We had to stay on top of it, and because I was not a great expert in these areas, we hired people to do it for us.

We used it to our advantage in another way, by communicating in a positive way to the recruits and our own players. We pushed things out there through social media and other websites. We did a tremendous amount of recruiting and promoting through social media. At Minnesota, we used it to really get the whole "Brick by Brick" theme out there, and it was a very positive way to operate.

Of course, social media affected our recruiting in less-than-desirable ways too. For example, in the past, we used to be able to hide a recruit. We would be able to bring in some outstanding football players that no one else had heard about. I loved to think about other teams in their meeting rooms saying, "Where did they find this guy? How come we didn't go after him?" Because of social media, there aren't as many of those conversations anymore.

In the old days, you had to work to find the good athletes, the great players. Today, all you have to do is push a button on the computer and the top 150 high school players will pop up on a screen. Things definitely have changed. Is it easier to find players to go look at? Yes, it is. But other teams find the same players that way.

I don't mean to say that hard work, scouting out players, and using all your contacts isn't still a part of it, but in many respects it puts those who don't work as hard on a similar playing field. And there is some unfairness to all that.

It is impossible to keep *anything* quiet. As soon as you talk to a player and leave his house, it is up on social media before you get to your car. Forget about coming back to school with the message, "You are not going to believe what I found in Mobile, Alabama." Kids post things, text each other, and tell everything. They want someone else to know that Notre Dame stopped by or that they just met with Coach Kill from Minnesota or Jim Harbaugh from Michigan. It's just the way it is, so we have to get used to it, accept it, and become better for it.

As I said, there is good and bad that goes with all of it. Social media can be used in a positive way, and then there are a lot of things that are on the negative side of it. When I first got to Minnesota, it was a big problem. It's actually hard to believe what kids will put out there for everyone to see. Some of the stuff we saw, we just said, "You've got to be kidding me. He put this out there?" I mean, someone is having a keg party and they put that out there for everyone to see, including their coaches? How dumb is that?

We brought experts in to talk to the team, individuals who had firsthand experience with something that had destroyed their lives. We also had people talk to our kids about how to use these methods of communication in positive ways. We educated them. We gave prime examples of people in high positions who should have known better but had ruined their lives by doing stupid things through social media. That stuff doesn't go away; it is out there forever.

We have one of our staff, Jeff Jones, who goes through social media and the media accounts of players who got in trouble and posts the story of what they did in the locker room for the players to see. It is amazing what kinds of trouble kids can get themselves into. And then I will spend time talking about the incidents with the kids. I'll tell them something like, "How in the hell can so and so—who is on a full scholarship and is one of the best players in the nation—do something like this? I mean, you have got to be kidding me!"

One day I was talking about the changes today in coaching and everything else because of social media, and I was asked how often I talked to the team about it. My answer was two words: "Every day!" Anytime I was around the kids—every day after practice, after meetings, during any communication time with the team—I brought it up. Their accountability was paramount. "Hey, we won today. Enjoy the win, but you be smart. Don't go out and do something stupid." Every day after I met with the team, I would end it with, "Do the right thing. Think about what you are doing and don't go out there and do something to get yourself in trouble."

I have a list of the top things that can get you in trouble in college football. They are drugs, alcohol, sexual harassment, social media, plagiarism, cheating on a test, stealing credit cards, and stealing from a teammate. I mean, if you stole from a teammate, you were gone for sure.

It seems like every year I would add to the list because of something stupid someone did. I know one of my additions one year was leaving the scene of an accident, because we had someone do that. I was fortunate not to have many of these incidents, and that was mostly due to the kind of kids we brought in, and because we were constantly reminding kids to do the right thing. We hammered this at them every single day.

We were not on the front page of the newspaper on a regular basis. Under my watch, we occasionally had some minor issues that we took care of right away. When I first got to the U of M, we had to clean up some things, but as I said, for the most part our kids stayed out of trouble.

I even worked with Hennepin County sheriff Rich Stanek in getting some horse barns cleaned up. We sent some guys out there to be with their officers and do some extra duties, as punishment. We felt after their assignments were completed they would give some serious thought to the next time a house party was on their agenda.

That was something that worked well for us. It taught the kids a lesson, got them up early in the morning, and initiated some positive contact with police officers. It also got work done that had to be done.

If after a football player leaves your school in five, four, or sometimes three years, they are a better person, then that's how you're graded. What kind of a coach have you been and what kind of an influence you have been on their life? That's all that counts. You know, that's how I always evaluated my performance.

I told parents all the time, "I'm going to take your kid from you, and I am going to make him better." My job was to take them to the next step. I wanted to make them professional students. I had to get them ready to be professional, and a good person, out in the real world.

There were a lot of things that we learned through the years to help our kids become better football players and better people, and how to handle social media was definitely one of them.

I WAS ASKED RECENTLY if I think I will ever use all these tools of my trade again someday, meaning, will I ever be a head football coach again?

I know I would truly enjoy being in a position as an associate athletic director over a football program. I know football will always be a part of my life, but I don't know how it will fit in. I might be on a selection committee somewhere, maybe a bowl game consultant, maybe a teaching football consultant, I don't know. I might consider a position coach someday. Do I ever want to be a head coach again? The answer is no. I was recently offered a head coaching job in Division I-AA and I knew that wasn't for me.

At this point I'm not ready to coach again. Like I said, I know for sure I will be a part of football again someday. I just don't know what part it will be.

| six |

Upsetting Cancer

THE VOCABULARY I USED and listened to during my days as a head football coach consisted of words and phrases such as option plays, quarterback sacks, rushing the passer, 4-3 defense, blocking kicks, and going for two points...those kinds of things. I wasn't prepared for the words renal cell carcinoma. *Cancer!*

I was coaching at Southern Illinois University, and toward the end of our game against Illinois State on October 15, 2005, I collapsed on the field with a seizure. I was taken to Carbondale Hospital and they really had a difficult time getting the seizure under control. I was struggling to breathe and not doing well.

The medical personnel could not handle what was going on with me, so I was flown by helicopter to a hospital in St. Louis, where they were finally able to get me stabilized. At the same time as all this was going on, I was also complaining about a tremendous amount of rib pain. I mean, the pain was just killing me. Apparently it was brought on by the violent seizure I had experienced.

While I was there they did some X-rays and the doctor told me, "Hey, we found a couple spots on your kidney, and you may want to get that looked at soon." So after I was stabilized, they sent me home, and I was soon back at SIU coaching again. But what the doctor had said was on my mind, so I thought, *Well, maybe I better go get those spots checked out.* So when I got a little time, I went in to the doctor in Carbondale and had an MRI. After the exam, I went back to work.

It wasn't too long after that I got a call. We were preparing for our next game, against Youngstown State. I was working with our offensive staff on the game plan and the phone rang. I went in and picked it up, and it was the doctor calling. He said to me, "Coach, I need you to come into the office tomorrow. I need to talk with you about something."

I said, "Hey, you can talk to me now. It's no big deal. I can hear what you have to say on the phone. I mean, I have a hundred things I'm doing right now preparing for our game this week. Really, Doc, you can tell me on the phone. What's going on?"

And he said, "Well…you've got cancer." "Cancer, really?" I said back to him. I said, "Doc, are you sure? Are you positive about that?" And he said, "Yes, I am. I'm sure that's what you have. You need to come and see me, and we need to talk about this as soon as possible." I said, "Okay."

I hung up the phone and went back to work. I didn't miss a beat. I didn't talk to anyone about it. We had work to do and had to put our game plan together. I didn't think about it. I was locked into what I was doing. It was about 6:00 in the evening, and we had about four more hours of work ahead of us.

On the way home, I started thinking about it. My mom happened to be in town with us, and I was worried about her because my dad had died of cancer and I wasn't sure what was ahead for me. I can remember thinking, *What am I going to say to my family about this when I get home?*

I got home and sat down with Rebecca, my mom, and my kids. It was not a good night for any of us. But I just told them straight out, "I got a call from the doctor today about those tests."

I remember someone—maybe Rebecca—said, "How did that go?" And I said, "Well, I'm not sure, but they said I've got cancer." And of course that word, *cancer*, is about as bad a word as can be said in our language. And we had just lost Dad to cancer, so it was devastating news.

I told everyone we did not know anything for sure yet but that I needed to go and meet with the doctor. I made the point that we should go in early to see him because I had a lot to get done for our upcoming game.

The next day, Rebecca and I went to see the doctor. I guess I had Stage 4 cancer. Rebecca says that's what it was, but I didn't quite get all that. I was in some kind of a fog. What I had never became quite clear to me.

I didn't really listen to what the doctors had to say. Everything from that point on was foggy. The one thing I do remember, though, is they said what I had was not the aggressive kind. It was a slow-growing cancer. So I thought at the time, *Well, I guess that's good.*

I also recall asking the doctor if I could still coach. We had a good team, and I wanted to know if I could remain coaching the rest of the year and then have it taken out. The doctor kind of paused and went, "Ahhhhhhhhhhh, well, how long is the end of the year?" And I said, "I don't know. I mean, hell, we maybe got a chance to win it all, which could mean quite a few more games." So he said, "All I can tell you is that we can watch it for now, but as soon as the season is over, you are going in right away."

As it turned out we got into the playoffs by beating Western Kentucky in a nationally televised game on a Thursday night. And then we lost the next game, so it took about another month before the season ended. And I remember meeting Rebecca as we were coming off the field and saying to her, "Well, now we are going to a real game day. Now we got a big game coming up."

I had been feeling really tired at the time. I think football saved my life. I had been so damn busy that I didn't have time to think about what was happening to me with the cancer and all. Mentally I was fine because the whole medical stuff was not on my radar. And that was a good thing. It kept me sharp and focused, but like I said, I was tired.

The first real time I thought about my cancer was after that last game, where we got beat, and we were on the plane going home. And then I started thinking, *Man, what is going to happen now? What is ahead for me and my family?* It was starting to register.

Our team chaplain, Roger Lipe, who has been such an inspiration for me, talked to me through everything. Eventually after I had been diagnosed, before the season ended, people found out what was happening. I remember Mike Reis, our play-by-play guy, came to me and said, "Coach, people need to know about what you are going through. It's important."

It was right around the holidays when I went in. It was in 2005, and I recall being in the hospital and watching Texas playing for the national championship in the Rose Bowl. I was in a couple days before January 1. My only thoughts were, *If I can get this surgery done and get back on the road for recruiting, it is going to be fine.*

The day I went for surgery, Rebecca, my mom, and my two daughters were there with me, along with Rebecca's brother Darrel and Patty, and my friend Roger Lipe. My brother, Frank, didn't come. He had been through my dad dying and just couldn't do it. I understood.

I remember kissing Rebecca and my girls and saying, "Well, its game day!"

Another interesting thing here, though, is that a couple weeks before the surgery, we purchased our lake home on Faith Drive. It was terrible, and Rebecca questioned me about it, saying, "Why do we want this awful place? I mean, it is just terrible." My response was, "Hell, if I'm going to die, I want to die on a lake. I always wanted to live on a lake, and here it is." And the best part of it was the location: Faith Drive. It couldn't get much better than that.

The surgery went okay, but the pain after was unbelievable. I was hurting like never before. I saw Rebecca right away when I woke up and told her I loved her and asked if everything was all right. The original plan was to take the kidney out, but they found out when they went in they only had to take part of the kidney. And they also found a spot on the other kidney, but that one was not malignant.

Rebecca told me it had gone well and they felt they had gotten all the cancer and were going to watch the other spot. I remember saying the very next day, "Look, I want out of this place. I'm not kidding. I can't stand it here. I want to go home!"

It wasn't in the cards. I was a mess. I had a catheter in me and some kind of drain or something sticking in my side. Still, I got to moving some after a couple days. And again, I told the staff I wanted out. I thought I knew about pain, but I found out I didn't, because when they pulled that thing out of my side, I thought the world had come to an end. It was just awful.

I was determined to go home. I wanted out, and the staff was saying I had to do this and that before I could go home. Well, the fact is, putting it bluntly, it took me three hours to finally be able to use the bathroom for its intended purposes. It was not a good time. Eventually I had no choice but to take charge. My mom had taken our car and brought the girls home, so we didn't have a car to leave in. I called Tracy Claeys and said to him politely, "Hey, Tracy, get your ass up here and pick us up. I'm getting out of this place!"

Rebecca was with me, and I told her we were going to go. I had had enough. You know, there is a time to take action. And I knew if I called Tracy, he was going to come. I was his boss. What was he going to say, no? I don't think so.

He was able to get a big car from one of the local dealers and started up to get me in St. Louis. I told the nurses and everyone, "I'm out of here." They were all great. They got me all checked out and everything, and Rebecca and I were ready and waiting for Tracy.

I was so ready to go, I didn't even get properly dressed. I still had my hospital garb on. So Tracy pulled up and we got in the car and headed for home. We got about halfway to Carbondale, and it was a deal where I said, "I'm hungry. I've been eating all that hospital food, and we need to stop." I told Tracy to pull over! And Tracy said, "What? Coach, what are you doing? You can't." And I said, "I don't care! Pull over!"

So we pulled over in Mount Vernon, Illinois, at a Chili's Grill & Bar. And I had on my slippers and my hospital clothes, and I was all bandaged up. I was quite a sight! So I limped in there and went over and sat down, and nobody in the place said a word. I said, "I just want a damn good bowl of soup. I want the best soup you got in this place." I know everybody in the restaurant was looking at us and thinking, *What the hell is going on here?*

I overheard a few people quietly whispering, "Hey, that's Coach Kill over there. Yeah, the guy in the slippers and pajamas. Wow, he looks like hell." But no one came up and said a thing so I just ate my soup and got out of there and back in the car, and we headed for home.

When we got home, I was in tough shape. I could barely walk, and there was a couch downstairs ready for me to sleep on. Our regular bed was upstairs, and I wanted to be in my own bed, so somehow I managed to get up those stairs. After a few days, I got out some and did some walking and was beginning to be on the mend.

I mentioned the hospital where I had the surgery was in St. Louis, Missouri. After the surgery, and of course before, we had to make the trip from home, which was about two hours each way. One day after we had made the trip several times, I said to Rebecca, "How can people do this, make this drive and do all the other things you have to do, if they don't have any money?" And it was this conversation that got us going with the Coach Kill Cancer Fund.

So anyway, the day after I got back from surgery in St. Louis, I was sitting in my chair at home and one of the coaches brought a recruit by to see me. His name was Justin Allen, and the coach brought him over to the house to visit with me. I was at the table in my pajamas, and I signed him on the spot. Later on he told me, "Coach, how could I not commit to a guy that just had surgery, leaves his bed from upstairs, and comes down and sits at the table and talks to ya? I got to play for a guy like that."

There was a night—I'm not sure when in the process it was, but it was well into it—when I just broke down. I had been pretty good at handling all I had been through, but for some reason it just hit me hard and I had to let it all out. I lost it.

I was thinking, *The seizure, cancer, all of it. What is ahead?* It was a tough moment. Rebecca was there with me, and she comforted me. I remember her telling me, "You'll be all right. You can coach and you can do all of it. It's going to be okay."

I got through it because of Rebecca. She was the rock. She has always been the rock in our family, and she pulled me through. Anytime you have someone you love by your side, it makes a big difference when you are going through tough times. She just had the answers to my questions and kept reassuring me that everything was going to be all right.

Roger Lipe was another one who helped me through. He is the best Christian man I know. He knows how to talk to you, how to relate to you, and he has the "it factor." He's a faith doctor. You have to have your medical doctors obviously, but Roger was a faith doctor for me. And then with my wife by my side too, it really helped me get through the difficult times.

I knew there were no guarantees; there still aren't. We don't know if the cancer will come back at some time. I'll talk more about the seizures later, but that one seizure I had saved my life. Because without it happening, they would never have found the cancer. Kidney cancer is very hard to find, and it is often too late once it is found.

I was also very stressed about my career at the time. I thought, *Should I keep coaching? Will I be able to give my best coaching all the time?* Those were things that were very troubling for me at the time. The bottom line is that I told the kids how they had to always give it their all, and then I wondered if I could still set the example for them. And if I couldn't, what kind of example would I be setting? Those were the troubling things for me. Could I do it the way I wanted to do it? Would I have the ability to coach the way I knew I had to coach? At the end of the day, those very thoughts ended my coaching at Minnesota.

I had to go back to St. Louis for regular checkups. And as I mentioned, it was on one of those trips that the conversation came up about people who didn't have the money to go through what I had gone through.

We had the means to do what needed to be done, including all the travel back and forth for diagnoses, checkups, and all those things. I just kept thinking, *How do people do this?* And then after thinking about it more, I said, "We need to do something about this."

I knew of people through college football who had started various kinds of foundations. And that's what I wanted to do. That's when I got connected with Woody Thorne, vice president of community affairs at Southern Illinois Healthcare (SIH), and he told me, "Coach, you don't have to do anything like starting your own foundation. You can do it right here with us. We can do it right here in southern Illinois, and we can run it right through our hospital system. We have it all in place. We can call it the Coach Kill Cancer Fund and run it right here through the hospital."

I thought this was great, but I was concerned about one thing. I didn't want the money to go to research or something like that, and I didn't want people to get funding in a hundred years or so. I wanted people who needed the money to get it *right now* and not have to wait for it. What I meant was to get the money in three or four days or sooner—maybe for gas money, for a babysitter, for a funeral, for cab fare, for those kinds of things.

I wanted immediate relief for the people who needed something right now. SIH was connected to people who didn't have health insurance and was able to reach out and assist them. So we just started it, and lo and behold, it got going and started working.

It raised a lot of money for southern Illinois but probably would not seem like a lot up in the Twin Cities, but we are still raising money. We are always trying to stay ahead of the curve, and to this point, the Coach Kill Cancer Fund has helped a lot of people.

Thank God for Woody Thorne, Paula Frisch, Gene Honn, and others who have been so active with the Coach Kill Cancer Fund and have kept it going. Rebecca has been very active going back and forth, and I try to go back for a fund-raiser once a year.

One thing the cancer really did for me was put life in perspective. I think by going through all this, especially with what happened to my dad, I thought, *I need to really get every single thing out of life I can get*. Because you don't know. You don't know what is going to happen and what the future holds for you and your family.

I always pushed myself hard, as well as people who worked for me and those I was around. But since the cancer, I think I even push harder for everyone to be the best they can be. It has all been put in perspective for my family and me. As far as work goes, I always tried to work harder than anyone I ever knew, but I think now I work even harder, which most certainly contributed to my problems after cancer (more on this to come). The body can only take so much, mentally and physically.

Because of all this, I think I am a better husband, a better father, and I don't take a thing for granted. Certainly my faith has become stronger. You know, life has a funny way of doing things. I mean, why would we go buy a lake house on Faith Drive just before my cancer surgery? Why would I think about starting a Coach Kill Cancer Fund? Why this? Why that?

We'd been driving around looking for a place for a couple years and couldn't find anything, and all of a sudden we found the place on Faith Drive, on Lake Egypt. We used to have a fishing tournament out that way to raise money, and so I had been around the area looking. The place we bought wasn't even for sale at the time. I met this older guy who told me about the place, and we ended up buying it. Lake Egypt is a lake I always wanted to be on, so it all worked out. Do I think we were supposed to buy a place on the lake of my dreams, on Faith Drive, before my surgery? I don't know. Maybe. But when I pull in down there on Faith Drive, I often think about it.

As I recovered from my surgery, it didn't take long for me to hit the road recruiting. I think it was only about six days before I was off with Matt Limegrover going after kids for our football team. He would go to the schools and I would go to the hotel. And I would lay there and relax, and then when he got back from the schools, we would go out to some home visits. And then we would do the same thing the next day and the day after that.

I had some problems in the area of my kidneys for a couple years after my surgery. I don't know exactly what it was, but it was a bothersome kind of hurt that just nagged at me. I guess it was normal for the kind of surgery I'd had, and eventually it went away. It probably was also aggravated some by my doing more than I was supposed to be doing during my recovery phases. But I had to recruit, so what the hell!

My philosophy was to keep busy and do what I had to do. I knew if I recruited the way I was supposed to do it, my mental attitude would be a positive for me and take my mind off the cancer. If I didn't, I would be worried about the cancer and even more about the recruiting, and that wouldn't be good for me at all.

When it comes to illnesses, I think the attitude is very helpful. You have to look at the positives and not the negatives. I have seen a lot of kids with serious problems who have found ways to deal with their problems by having a great attitude. Dan O'Brien's high school son, Casey, has that mental approach. He has a rare form of cancer that is very aggressive. When I see what Casey has gone through and how he has fought what he has with a great attitude, it is unbelievable.

When I talk with people I really stress the mental aspect. You can't get down on what is going on, and you must keep a good attitude and look forward to positive things in your life. The more positive you are and the more you force yourself to do things, the better off you will be. When you get old, you may really have to force yourself to walk. And you must do that. Get out of bed every day and look forward to the day ahead of you. Keep that positive attitude. It works.

Lance Armstrong had a book out called *Live Strong* at the time I was recovering from cancer and I read it and thought it was helpful. Anything you can do during tough times to keep your mental approach moving in the right direction will help you, no doubt.

Dan Callahan was the baseball coach at Southern Illinois University when I was there coaching football, and we became great friends. He and I were diagnosed with cancer at around the same time.

We would drive around campus and talk. I would ask him questions about how he was doing, and he would do the same with me. I would say to him, "Hey, don't ever give in. Stay positive and keep doing what you love to do." I told him, "Keep busy. Try not to think about it, because the more you can do that, the better chance you will have to enjoy your life." And he did that. He continued to coach baseball almost right up to the end, maybe a month or a month and a half before he passed.

I think it was all the medicine and everything else that was going on that eventually brought him down to where he couldn't do much. He was going downhill and he knew it, so it was tough. Roger Lipe came in and spent a lot of time with Dan, and I know that helped, because it sure did with me.

As bad as Dan got toward the end, never once did he say anything about dying. Maybe he did to Roger, but I never heard it come out of his mouth. And as a result of his attitude toward everything, he was able to do a lot of things and enjoy much of his life even during the worst of times for him and his family. When it was his time, he was prepared to go. He fought it and got everything he could out of life before it was time. He was like Dad in many ways, refusing to let cancer whip his ass. His attitude kept him going. I miss him.

I often have told those with serious conditions that there is only one person who is going to control what is happening to you, and that's not any of us. It's the man upstairs. And the man upstairs tests the strong, and you have got to stay strong. Don't give in to the damn stuff. Keep moving and doing what you can do until you can't do it anymore. And then when that point arrives, find something that can take your mind off what is happening. Don't sit in a chair and think about dying. Think about living one day at a time, and get as much out of that day as you can.

A short time ago, I had a meeting with a young lady named Mia Gerold; she was nine years old when we first met. This little girl was connected to me by one of our players at U of M, Josh Campion. He came to me one day and said, "Coach, I know you had cancer, and I know this little girl who has it too." Before he went any further, I told him to have her come up to the office so I could meet her.

So she came up to see me, and you would never in a million years know she had cancer. She had this beautiful curly hair and was bouncing around my office like nothing was wrong. She came up and sat on my lap and had the most unbelievable attitude.

I remember she was wearing this shirt that said OUT OF LIFE on it. I said to her, "Mia, what does that mean on your shirt?" She said,

"Coach, I'm getting everything out of life that I can get!" And she did. She had been diagnosed with terminal brain cancer. Her mom told me she maybe had six months left, and you would never have known it. I mean, she had a super duper attitude, just like Casey O'Brien. He would get done with his chemo treatments and then the next day be playing in a golf tournament. Those are stories you can share with other people. Those who are ill want to hear real-life stories, not a bunch of bullshit!

For some reason the particular tumor she had has gone away. We stay in touch, and she is now 15 years old. She is a miracle child, no doubt about that. And with her, as long as I have known her, it is attitude, attitude, attitude! She is the little girl who ran out of the tunnel with me at Minnesota before our home opener against New Mexico State. It was a great moment I will never forget sharing with her.

Sam Sigelman, an attorney, came to see me one day. He said, "Hey, Coach, I've got cancer. What's it like?" I told him, "Keep it positive. Go after your life and do what you can, but never give in to it. Keep that positive attitude." He had this new kind of surgery and he survived it and is very successful. It's those kinds of stories that keep you going. Move ahead. Kick cancer right in the face!

It's been a little more than 10 years since I was diagnosed with cancer, and for the most part I haven't had any real setbacks. I have pretty much been able to do what I wanted to do and kept that positive attitude. With cancer, you pretty much know what you have and how it's going to be treated.

I truly believe I developed cancer for a reason. It was supposed to happen to me. I was able to start a cancer fund and I have been able to help other people along the way. It has given me a whole new perspective on life.

God has a plan. I have said that perhaps cancer and epilepsy have been the best things that ever happened to me. I'm not invincible; I found that out, and then I was able to give back to others who needed it. And I think, as I mentioned before, it has made me a better husband, better father, better son, better brother, and better person in general.

I think I became a better coach, and the kids played their asses off for me because of the cancer and epilepsy. I think I am more driven to be the best. I think I communicate better. I think I instill things better in people, such as, "You have this one day today, with no promises for tomorrow, so give it all you got."

The kids I coached at the time knew I had cancer. When they saw it didn't change any way that I coached except for the fact that I gave *even more*, I think it inspired them. I really believe that. It was like, "Hey, if the old man can give that much, we sure can."

I think I live a different philosophy than most people with all this. I think you can go to all the doctors in the world, but the fact is, as my dad used to say, "When your card comes up, it comes up." And so you better be ready. And with that thought, I made sure I got right with God, with the church, and did a lot of things differently.

We made the decision to become catholic as a family after Dad died. We went to classes every Wednesday night. I can recall when I told the coaches, Matt Limegrover said, "There is no way he is going to leave a meeting with us on a Wednesday night to do that." But I did, and I am grateful for doing it. It helped my faith considerably. It changed our lives.

My kids handled the cancer and everything else very well. Kids in general are relentless and resilient. I think they knew me well enough to always know, "Dad is going to find a way. Just like he will find a way to win a football game, he will find a way to beat this." And I did.

As I said, Rebecca has always been the rock in our family. She tells me all the time that I am the rock, but really she is. She had to raise the kids and take them all over the place while I was coaching, and she did a tremendous job in every respect. She is the one who is the foundation behind my attitude and "moving forward" approach to life. Dan Callahan and I became close through the relationship Rebecca formed with Dan's wife, Stacy, and their girls. And she and Stacy are still best friends. Rebecca is the rock for me and for too many others to even begin to mention.

Through the advice I have given people, I have grown. I know you have to have faith and you have to believe you can beat anything. Don't feel sorry for yourself, because all you have to do is look around and you will find someone worse off than you. Don't surround yourself with anything that is negative, because it will bring you down. Concentrate on you and what you have to do to get better. Get a doctor you are comfortable with and who you bond with, because this is your life on the line. Make sure you take care of your body. Make sure what you put in it, you get out of it.

I think Casey O'Brien has done a good job with that. He changed his diet. He understands that eating right and getting enough sleep can make a difference. He is a living example. It gives you a chance when you do things right. Casey had a goal to play football and now the doctors told him he can't. So what did he do? He said, "Well, then I will be a holder for field goals and extra points." So he got out of the hospital, and three days later he was the holder for his high school football team in a game. And that was his goal.

Some thought Casey's dad was crazy for letting him do that. Why? No one knew what was going to happen. If he wanted to hold the football and the doc said okay, let's let him hold it and hope he doesn't get hit. Why not? Why shouldn't he have had the chance to do that? He got some golf clubs and is working at that. If he can't play football, then he'll play golf.

Now he is looking at college and wants to be a holder for the football team. Three or four colleges are on his radar, and he has asked my help to communicate his story to the coaches at those schools. This kid wants to be a holder, and with his great attitude he will be successful.

Todd Oakes, the assistant baseball coach at Minnesota, and Connor Cosgrove, a former Gophers wide receiver, are both great examples of not letting an illness get in the way of having a tremendous and courageous attitude. These are special people who find ways to move ahead, and always in a positive direction.

I have always felt that I probably brought on all my physical problems by not taking care of myself right, by not getting enough sleep, not eating right, going a hundred miles an hour all the time, and basically not watching out for myself. Rebecca has often told me, "You always worry about taking care of all the people in the world, but you don't take care of yourself."

I suppose some of the disease is probably inherited, because there have been a lot of people on my dad's side who have had cancer, but for me to move ahead, I know I need to practice just exactly what I tell others. And I'm working on it every day.

A lot hit me when I found out about the cancer. I learned a great deal about myself and about life. I know how much it hurt not to be able to do things I wanted to right away. In fact, when I was in the hospital for the surgery, it killed me that I could not go to Krystal's senior volleyball game. There I was, laying in the hospital, and I couldn't do what I wanted to do. I couldn't go to my daughter's important volleyball game. It killed me!

So you know what? My football team went in my place. Can you believe that? That's the kind of guys we had on our team. They went in my place. It's those kinds of things that really can change you and give you a perspective on life, on people, and on all of its importance. I will never forget that.

It's all about caring for others and caring for yourself. Take care of yourself, and above all, no matter what life has in store for you, your attitude will get you through.

| seven |
Attacking Epilepsy

I WAS A FOOTBALL COACH for 32 years. I didn't have time to think about anything else. I had a little detour with cancer along the way, and then epilepsy came along and really threw me off course.

Up to the point when it hit me, I didn't know very much about epilepsy. I had heard of the disease, I guess pretty much like everyone else, but that was about it. I was uneducated when it came to epilepsy. I guess I thought it was kind of like cancer, MS, and other illnesses of that nature, but I probably knew even less about epilepsy because it wasn't talked about as much as some of the more common illnesses.

I just figured the disease was different from some others, but I really didn't know how different. The first real connection I had to it was back when I was coaching at Emporia State. And I'm not sure you could even call it a connection. Anyway, I had what I will call an episode.

I was getting out of bed one morning and going to take a shower, and I ended up on the floor. I must have hit my head as I fell. We had a friend, Sarah Everson, who we were helping out by letting her live with us, and she found me. I was taken to the hospital and had a bunch of tests that apparently showed I had some kind of lesion on my brain. They thought this might have been what caused the fall and possible seizure. But I was never convinced it was a seizure and prefer calling it an episode because there was no evidence to the contrary, only speculation.

The follow-up was for me to take medication, which I took for a while and then moved on. I do recall falling in the shower one time when I was at Pittsburg State too. But again, I never thought it was seizure-related. With both these incidents, I was too busy coaching to let it bother me, and I forged ahead. It was later on, after the seizure at Southern Illinois, that I began to learn more.

Some seizures are called tonic-clonic seizures or grand mal seizures. I supposedly had that. I don't remember any advanced warning—feeling funny or anything like that before it happened. I have never felt one coming on. I guess some people do, but it hasn't been that way for me.

When it came on for me at Southern Illinois, I was taken to the hospital and I was really struggling. I wasn't coming out of it, so they took me to St. Louis by helicopter. I know from being told later that what I had was very serious, and people can die from similar kinds of seizures.

While at the hospital in St. Louis they were able to get it controlled. They actually tried to make me have more seizures in order to determine why it happened. I saw a neurologist there, and they tried lots of things. I recall them putting electrodes in my head and trying to trace what was happening to me during the episodes.

It was at that time that they checked my ribs, because they were so sore, and they found the cancer. All they told me about what got me to the hospital was that I had had a seizure. No one mentioned anything to me about epilepsy. Nothing like that registered with me, either. The focus for me at that point was solely on the cancer.

Later on I was told if a person has one incident, it is called a seizure, and more than one is potentially epilepsy. However, it can be difficult to determine at first. There are all kinds of seizures. I was told there are seizure disorders, epileptic seizures, and seizures from stress, such as those suffered by returning war veterans. It is important to be sure seizures are epileptic in nature and not caused by some other stimulus before one is determined to have epilepsy.

While at Southern Illinois I had more seizures, but only that one actually occurred on the field. I try to forget about the past, but I would say I probably had about three total there. I know there was one that happened in the office. They were all serious ones, the tonic-clonic kind. So in 2007 I was put on another medication, called Keppra. It's the kind of medication that can make you really high-strung, moody, and tired.

When I was hired at Northern Illinois in 2008, Jim Phillips, the athletic director, never asked me a question about the seizures. I knew he knew about them, but we never discussed them at the time. He just hired me because he knew I could coach football and knew how to win.

While at Northern Illinois, the seizures continued and I had a few at different places, maybe one per year. In total, there might have been three or four. Two were at the house, and I think one was after a bowl game. There is no way to determine why some seizures are worse than others. One of the two that occurred at our house was a really bad one. It lasted about 45 minutes, and I was taken to Northwestern Hospital in Chicago. I know I got there because of Jim Phillips, who helped me out with his connections.

I was not in good shape after those incidents. When the seizures were over, and especially the next day, I was extremely sore and it took a significant amount of time to recover fully. I mean, a bad one like the one I just mentioned was like being in a car wreck. My body felt like it had taken a terrible beating. I was very tired after and felt totally worn-out. Mentally, I just kept going. I tried not to let it affect me.

The only thing that really bothered me was how this was going to affect my coaching. Would I have to quit coaching? How bad were these going to get? What did the future hold? Those thoughts were in my mind but not for long; I had too much to do.

I seemed to be able to recover and just get back to work. There was a time, though, while at Southern Illinois, when after a bad one I just finally lost it. I told Rebecca, "You know, this is just crazy. I can't keep going through this." I just broke down and was really depressed. And then, like most other roadblocks that have come along in my life, I moved on.

I think all this hurt and scared Rebecca much more than me. Sure, I was depressed after knowing these things had happened to me, but I had never seen one occur, so I didn't really know what the experience was like for someone else. Rebecca was involved firsthand, so she knew the seriousness of what was happening with me.

With most seizures I am unconscious. I don't recall anything about the one that occurred on the sideline at Southern Illinois until I woke up in the hospital in St. Louis. That's how out of it I am when it happens.

Epilepsy is a different kind of disease. As I said, I have never seen a seizure, and the closest I have gotten to it is what Rebecca has described for me. It's a deal where, again, with coaching I never had time to think about it. I didn't talk to people about it outside the family. No one ever said anything to me personally. I would talk to Rebecca about it and she would tell me things, and I would just cringe and say "God," and then move on. I just never let it get to me. I am pretty strong in that regard, and I guess it was a good thing I was living my dream as a football coach, because that was where my mind was the majority of the time.

No matter how things were going, we were never told exactly how to handle my seizures. After having one, I would walk away from it and forge ahead. What I did do, though, was go to several different neurologists, trying to find out what was causing the seizures. I couldn't get an answer about the cause, because there is no answer. That's the problem; it is one of those deals where you have the unknown.

Epilepsy is not like cancer. Cancer can be pretty well defined, and you know what, where, and why. With epilepsy, it is not that way, and that's what makes it so hard to deal with. You never know when it is going to hit you.

While at Northern Illinois, I know the generic medicine I took caused some problems because of its strength level compared to the regular medicine. This threw me for a loop, so I had to get that straightened out.

When I was coaching, I never told coaches what to do if I had a seizure. I never talked about it to them and just went about my job coaching the football team. My attitude with it up to that point was pretty simple: have the incidents, recover from them the best I could, and move on. I was not going to let them interfere with what I had to do...even though they were becoming a huge interference.

At Northern Illinois I kept moving ahead. I was having great success coaching, and our teams were outstanding. I had a great coaching staff, loved the area where we were living, and enjoyed my life. My family was all great, the kids were doing well, and Rebecca was always right there by my side, which made everything just fine.

And then, with all that going on, Minnesota called. At the time, there were some other schools that had sought me out, and Rebecca and I had some discussions about going to those places. But I had not ever considered Minnesota until Joel Maturi called me. When we talked, the question about my epilepsy never came up in the conversation. I mentioned earlier that when we met at an airport restaurant, the only thing that came up was a question about my overall health. I told Maturi I was doing good, feeling good, and so on, because at that time I was.

When I was offered the job at Minnesota, we never had any family discussions about whether I shouldn't take the job because of the epilepsy. We never discussed the bigger stage, the more stress that might be involved, or anything like that. It seemed like a great opportunity to go to the Big Ten conference, and we took it.

My health issues, including the seizures in the beginning, were more of an annoyance than anything else. They kept me off the field, and I didn't like it. Still, after all I had gone through to that point and over the coming years, I only missed one football game. My mind was on football, not something I didn't even understand.

Before Minnesota, we never spent any time trying to find out what was going on with me. For me, my take on it was a "seizure disorder." I never called what I had epilepsy. I said it must be a seizure disorder from fatigue.

I had a couple doctors tell me a few things about what I had, in St. Louis and again at Northwestern, but to be honest, I never paid any attention to what they said. I didn't have time for all that. I mean, if no one else in the medical profession could really understand and explain the whats and whys, how was I supposed to get it?

For me it was simple. As I mentioned, I figured I overworked myself, never got much sleep, my body would get tired and run down, and I would have a seizure. It was more of a mental thing in my brain—at least that was my take on it.

There are some among my family and friends who did feel that my workload would be greater. I never felt that way. I was always up for any challenge. At Southern Illinois, I collapsed on the field, and at Northern Illinois I had the seizures but not as publicly. But how would it be at Minnesota, where I was more in the spotlight with the massive media market in the Twin Cities?

When I had my first seizure there—at least that people knew about—my first year at Minnesota, it got a lot of attention. And there was a woman—Vicki Kopplin, the head of the Epilepsy

Foundation in Minnesota—who wanted to get to me and talk to me.

She wanted me to get involved with the Epilepsy Foundation and be kind of a figurehead for the organization, that kind of thing. Initially I thought, *I'm not doing that. I will lose my job. If people know all about my history, it won't be good.*

Well, Vicki didn't give up. She kept at me. I mean, she kept trying to get an appointment to see me for about two years. She had been very persistent, and finally I agreed to talk with her. I gave her 15 minutes. She was telling me about this gala that was coming up and how I could help all these people. She went on about how I could be a great ambassador for epilepsy, and she was very persuasive.

Finally I said, "Okay, I'll go to the gala." So I went to the gala to help them raise money. At the event they had adults and kids speak about epilepsy and things they had gone through, and I thought, *Wow, this is something to hear all these people.* I thought, *How good do I have it?* What I heard about some of the kids was just terrible. With their problems, their future was so bleak. It really hit me hard. I felt so bad for some of the people who were there.

I spoke at the event and I told Vicki I would help her, and we became a team. It wasn't long before people were reaching out to me for advice. I met a lady named Deb Hadley whose daughter had died of epilepsy. And she wanted to get it out there that people were dying from this disease. I met her after her daughter died, and she just wanted to talk to someone. I was there for her and was really moved by her experience.

This was kind of how it all began with the Coach Kill Chasing Dreams Epilepsy Fund. I give Vicki all the credit. There is another person named Mark Evenstad, a great donor, who was influential in getting our fund going.

Rebecca was instrumental in starting the Go-Pher Epilepsy Awareness Game at TCF Bank Stadium—a game that strives to bring awareness to epilepsy—and it really got things rolling for the foundation. Eventually, down the road a ways, this connection ended up saving my life.

At Minnesota, there was no question I was on the big stage. Everything I did was evaluated and scrutinized. It has been my practice that I never personally follow what the media says or writes. I don't read it and I don't watch it. But I do have someone who checks it for me, mostly to be sure if I am quoted, it is the right quote. The reason I stay away from it is that I feel the media has the right to say what they want to say. And I was told a long time ago that if you are going to worry about what everyone says about you, it isn't going to help you. As a coach, it seems best to put yourself in a bubble and worry about your football team and nothing else. If you don't read or listen to the media, what you don't know isn't going to hurt you.

Probably the only exception for me is things written by Sid Hartman of the *Star Tribune*. Sid has been around so long, and we have such a good relationship, that I totally trust him. Sid might stop by with an article he wants me to read, and I'll do it because it's Sid asking or giving me something to read.

There was one writer who did get to me some with something he wrote. It was an article by Jim Souhan of the *Minneapolis Star Tribune* that ran on September 15, 2013. Souhan said some pretty nasty things about me without any personal knowledge of what I was going through at the time. (Since the article, Rebecca and I have made amends with Jim and moved on.)

The article came after the Western Illinois game, when I had a seizure on the sideline. It was a Tuesday, and I was back at work getting ready for practice. I had put my practice clothes on and walked out, and there was no one in the office or anywhere around. Something was going on, but I didn't know what. So I went to the players' lounge and saw some people there watching something on the television.

The program was *Outside the Lines*, and they were talking about me and a sportswriter from Minnesota. I couldn't figure out what was going on. Why were they talking about me on that program? There were some national figures talking about Jim Souhan and blasting him, and I thought, *What the hell am I doing on* Outside the Lines, *and what does this have to do with Souhan?*

Someone then told me there was an article in the paper that Souhan had written about me. When practice was over, Jim came over to me and said he wanted my reaction to his article. He never really apologized, and I told him, "Jim, you can write whatever you want and say what you want. I can't do anything about that. If there comes a time when I feel I can't coach the game, then I'll walk away." Well, I hadn't read the article yet.

When I got home that night, I said to Rebecca, "What do you know about this article by Jim Souhan?" And she said, "You don't want to read it." I told her, "Well, Jim Souhan came up to me after practice and kind of wanted to talk about it." So I then read the article, and my first reaction was, "You've got to be kidding me! He has no idea what I've been through."

The article basically said I was an embarrassment to the university and no one should have to watch someone "flipping around on the ground." I mean, it was brutal. I recall saying, "Man, he has offended every disabled person in America." And that's when the fireworks started. I never talked to him after that, until recently.

After the article, I got letters, and people contacted me from all over the country. It was absolutely unbelievable the people who reached out to me because of the article. I had so much support from people. There were people who privately told me they had epilepsy but had not revealed it to anyone out of fear of losing their jobs and friends.

I was angry and also offended for all the other people who Souhan had attacked with his article. My reaction was not good, I admit that, but I didn't let it eat at me. I mean, what was I going to do?

As I look back, Souhan's article did more for epilepsy than a hundred good articles. He brought more awareness to epilepsy than could ever have been imagined. There is no doubt that because I was on a big stage, it got so much more attention. If I had been a normal person, little likely would have been said after the fact. Because I was a major college football coach, the attention to the article was so much greater, and the effect it had on people was unbelievable.

My feeling about all this—whether it was the Souhan article or some other disruption, such as my medical issues—was to deal with it and get back to coaching. I had issues with the epilepsy several times while at Minnesota. There was one early on in the first year, and then a problem during halftime at Michigan State later on. The ones I had were not good. They lasted for some time and then continued back to back to back, that kind of thing. During all this, at times I had trouble with the medicines, and it was just a rough time for my family and me.

There were a significant number of seizures that occurred during the off-season too. I have also been told of some staring-type seizures where I didn't know really what was going on.

During the Michigan week, I was preparing for the game in my usual way. I felt really tired all week but was moving ahead with our game preparations. I recall coming home on Thursday night after practice, and everything seemed okay. On Friday I was at home and started having seizures. They weren't the long 30-minute ones but lasted only five minutes or so, and then I would go right into another one, over and over. I was not coherent from Friday until well after the game was over.

When they started happening on Friday, our trainer came over to see me and then a doctor I had seen came to the house. Rebecca had been in contact with Dan O'Brien, and the plan was to find a way to get me to the game in Ann Arbor once I was okay.

Well, I never got okay. At one point I kind of came around and saw my clothes hanging out for the game, and I asked Rebecca what was going on. She said something like, "It's okay; just get your rest and then we are going to get you to the game."

Well, I never did come around until Saturday night. I was out of it all that time and maybe had as many as 16 to 20 seizures. When I finally did come around, as I said, it was Saturday night.

I asked Rebecca what day it was. She said, "Saturday." I said, "Saturday! I'm supposed to be at the game." And she said, "Jerry, you didn't get to go to the game." I felt terrible. "I didn't get to go to the game? I missed the Michigan game?" I started crying and was as emotional as I had ever been. And then I went right back into a seizure again.

The next day, Jill Gattone—the wife of Phil Gattone, the president and CEO of the national branch of the Epilepsy Foundation—happened to be in town for a golf tournament. Rebecca called Vicki, the head of the local organization, and both Vicki and Jill came right over to our house.

When Jill arrived, she said immediately, "We have to get Jerry somewhere right now. He is in real trouble." So they got on the phone and got information that the two best doctors for epilepsy in the country were in Grand Rapids, Michigan, and Miami, Florida. We decided to go see Dr. Brien Smith in Grand Rapids. I really didn't know all that was going on because I was still out of it and actually still having seizures.

Dan O'Brien was able to get ahold of Dick Ames, one of the university donors, who let us use his private jet to get me to Grand Rapids. University president Eric Kaler, who succeeded Bob Bruininks in 2011, and our athletic director, Norwood Teague, came over to see how I was doing and told me to do what I had to do to take care of the problems.

I was in a condition like I was being detoxed. Rebecca and Dan were with me on the way to the airport. I just don't remember much of anything other than sweating profusely and feeling terrible. When we got to Grand Rapids, they kind of snuck me in the back door and up to where I was supposed to be. It was there I met Dr. Brien Smith.

When I got in there, they hooked me up with electrodes in my head and got me laying down and actually strapped me down so I couldn't move. When I had to go to the bathroom I wore a harness with a nurse by my side. It was about as uncomfortable a time as I have ever had. It wasn't a good place to be.

My mind was not anywhere. I was in a fog. I don't think at that time I had given a thought to much of anything. I had missed the Michigan game, and that was a big deal, but I'm not sure I was giving any thought to that at all. As I said, I was in a fog from all the seizures I had been having, plus all the medications they had me on.

While I was there, in addition to all the tests, a sleep doctor came in to evaluate me to see where I was with all that part of my life. Once I was coherent, Rebecca and I got a several-day educational seminar on epilepsy. We learned about every kind of seizure and how they related to me. We got a tremendous education— something we had never gotten from anyone in the past.

Dr. Smith and Dr. Ardeshna, his assistant, went over epileptic seizures, nonepileptic seizures, and other related things. They told us that some people have both, and I was somewhere in the middle. They told us what they were going to do. I had been on so many different drugs, it was like I was an addict. Dr. Smith's plan was to get me off what I had been on, and then to try this and try that until they found something that would work for me. As I said, it was almost like I was going through some kind of drug rehab.

That was the toughest thing I have ever faced mentally. The cancer was nothing compared to that. I was a really sick guy. I could barely move, I was tired, I was depressed, and I cried a lot with Rebecca by my side.

I remember talking to the coaches and trying to be a part of the next game plan. Maybe the worst part was not knowing what was going to happen to me. And I hated the depression; it made everything worse.

The doctors did a great job of explaining everything to me, which had never been done to that level in the past. The bottom line with me was that I was not getting any sleep. I was doing everything at the university. I was speaking all over. I was fund-raising. I was into all kinds of things, and I was coaching a Big Ten football team. My body, physically and mentally, couldn't take it anymore. I had been skipping meals on top of everything else, and then the medicines I was taking were not right for me. This caused me to be moody and on edge all the time. I was a mess.

Once I got on the right medicine, Rebecca told me it was like being married to a new person because of all the past side effects I had from the other drugs. I remember once my brother, Frank, had come up for the Western Illinois game, and I was so out of it with my moods that he couldn't take it and went home. It was great to finally be on the correct medications.

Again, I got an invaluable education while in Grand Rapids with Dr. Smith. I was told to get a sleep doctor involved with me when I got home. They also told me to get into a regular exercise routine.

We got home Thursday afternoon, and I was in better shape. We were advised that it may be that I was having two different types of seizures, epileptic and nonepileptic. One can be treated and the other cannot. The nonepileptic seizures are the ones I mentioned earlier that returning soldiers can have. Stress can cause them, and they can be caused by something really bad happening in a person's life going back many years.

All the other times I had had problems, I always saw a neurologist. Dr. Smith was an epileptologist, a doctor who specializes in epilepsy. He had epilepsy and had wanted to be a surgeon. But because he could not do that, he became an expert in the field of epilepsy. He and I hit it off well. He had played football, so we got along well and even had some great football discussions about players, teams, and so on. He was a great guy who gave us what we needed. I would tell anyone who has epilepsy—or any medical issue, for that matter—to find someone you trust. That is the most important thing you can do for yourself. And I trusted Dr. Smith.

Once I got back, I was not thinking anything about the game coming up. It was Friday, and we were scheduled to play Northwestern in Evanston the next day, but I was so tired. I didn't know what I was going to do. I thought I should go over to practice. So Rebecca drove me over to campus, and the team was going through their walk-through in preparation for Northwestern the next day. They finished up and I walked out on the field, and you could hear a pin drop.

I remember I told them it was great to see them, that I was proud of them. I told them I was sorry for what they had gone through and that I appreciated each of them. I also told them I could give them three examples of where I was at, and that it was caused by all the things I had been telling them to do that I was not doing. I said, "You have got to get enough sleep. You have to eat right. And if you have to be on medications, then be sure you are on the right ones, because those three things have taken me down. This is a great lesson for you." I went on to tell them, "There were two things I thought about while laying in that hospital, and I want you to take those two things with you tomorrow to Northwestern. And they are to play hard and have fun!"

That whole thing of being there with my team out on the field was very hard for me, and then I walked out. Rebecca and I left the field and went home. Later that afternoon, we decided we should go to the game. Rebecca said to me, "You know, you are not going to be able to do this." I said, "What do you mean?" And she told me, "You are not going to be able to sit here and watch the game. Are you feeling well enough to go?" I wasn't sure. That gives you an idea of how I was feeling at the time. All the times in the past I had dismissed what was happening to me and just moved ahead. I had said many times, "I have a football team to coach. I can't let these things bother me. I don't have time." All those thoughts, all those statements about putting those things in the rearview mirror and getting back to coaching, and now I didn't know if I could go to the game at Northwestern? I guess we all realized how really bad things had gotten.

My mom was with us in Minnesota at the time, and they put me in the backseat of the car and off we went to Evanston for the Northwestern game. Rebecca drove and I slept in the backseat and listened to the Cardinals game on the radio. Our plan was to go three-quarters of the way and stay overnight in a hotel, and if I had any problems we would either go back home or just stay at the hotel. I didn't tell anyone I was coming, in case I didn't make it.

We arrived at the hotel about midnight, and I was tired but doing okay. That night everything went well, so the next morning when we got to Evanston, everything was set for me to get into the stadium unnoticed for the most part. Adam Clark from my staff did an outstanding job of making all the arrangements for me to get up to the coaches' box through a back way. All of Adam's efforts worked perfectly.

I didn't see the players, just went to the coaches' box. When I came in, the coaches just kind of looked at me in shock. I told them right away, "Just coach." I sat in the second row and was involved in the game and contributed what I could.

The game was close, and when halftime arrived, I decided to go down to the locker room with the coaches. When the kids saw me, their eyes lit up and it was a lot of, "Hey, Coach," that kind of thing going on. They couldn't believe I was there, and I think it helped them.

We won the game, and to me, that game right there turned our season around the rest of the year. I think in the kids' minds it was probably something like, "If that old SOB can drive here to the game, then we can play!"

From there on, I was supposed to slow down, so I did some. But only *some*. I mean, instead of working 16 hours a day, maybe I worked only 10. I was still in every meeting and did all the things I was supposed to do as a head football coach. I simply didn't know any other way.

I might come in a little later in the morning if I was sleeping. Rebecca knew how important sleep was for me, so sometimes she would let me sleep a little more. I might get to the office at 7:30 AM instead of 6:00 AM.

Coach Tracy Claeys had been the acting head coach at the Northwestern game, and I decided for the rest of the season I would coach from the press box. I know there was some thought out there that I was not involved and that Tracy was the head coach at the time, but that was not true. I was the head coach. And saying that, I'm not trying to take anything away from Tracy, because he did a great job. But I was the head coach. And I do think it helped both the team and me at that time to be in the press box for the games. Hell, I'm not so sure I'm not a better coach from the press box. You certainly can see the game better than from down on the field, which is probably the worst seat in the house.

I enjoyed being up there, and we really went on a roll the rest of the season, beating Nebraska and Penn State and finishing a good year. That part of it went well, and things were going well for me. I was feeling good and went seizure-free for almost two years. I wanted to show Jim Souhan and everyone in the state that I was doing good and could coach at the major college football level.

I credit Dr. Smith with all that went well. He saved my life. I would never have been able to coach another two years without him. He taught me about the epilepsy and all that went with it. He told me I was going to be making life decisions for myself and my family. He said, "You have got to figure out what is best for you and for your wife and kids, and if you think coaching college football is part of it, then you need to do what you got to do."

As bad as things got for me and as serious a state as I was in, I honestly don't think there was a time when I thought I should quit coaching. It had been my life. I knew my back was against the wall. I knew if I wanted to coach I was going to have to take care of myself and do what I was told to do to keep my body and my mind right.

Before I ever got to the Michigan situation, I had had other struggles, but no one other than Rebecca really knew much about them. I had seizures at other times that were kept quiet. I recall one before an Iowa game that no one knew about. But believe me, I knew missing a game was a big deal.

I know others made a huge deal out of it too, but on the other hand there have been other big-time coaches who have sat out whole seasons because of medical issues. Urban Meyer did it for a whole year, and Coach Mark Dantonio was out three weeks once at Michigan State, so I wasn't the only one with medical issues.

My time in Grand Rapids with Dr. Smith saved my life. I felt pretty good again and was taking care of myself, and I was ready to get back to doing what I do: coaching football.

BEFORE I LEAVE THIS PART of my life regarding my battle with epilepsy, there are a few things I want to share that hopefully will help people better understand the disease and assist others who have epilepsy or who are close to someone who has epilepsy.

I have had a lot of positives in my life because of epilepsy. I think probably the biggest positive I have gotten is that I have been able to visit with so many people—not only in the state of Minnesota but throughout the country—about the issues they have. And they've reached out to me. They say things like, "Coach, what should I do? What do you think about these medications? What are you on? What doctor do you see?" A lot of them have never heard of an epileptologist, and I have been able to share that with them.

I have been able to get people headed in the right direction, and then on the other hand I have gotten a lot of notes from people and encouragement for my situation. So it kind of works back and forth, and for me that has been a big positive in my life.

Another positive is that I have been able to connect with Dr. Brien Smith and Phil and Jill Gattone, and I have become kind of a spokesman for epilepsy and been able to tell more people about the disease. I have been able to use the platform I am on in a positive way to get the word out. I think everything in life happens to you for a reason. The relationships I have built with kids and adults have allowed me to meet some incredible people through epilepsy. I have met people who are doing amazing things. You know, I met a young lady named Channing who has a dog named Georgia, and Channing is an equestrian rider with epilepsy. She has this thing around her in case she falls, and she is a big-time rider. Even with what she has, she is successful. I see this all the time meeting these kinds of special people who are doing special things.

I think the toughest part is to see people who will never be able to succeed. They have huge disabilities, cognitive issues, and they can't do much of anything. It is so sad. I have spoken at a lot of places and signed autographs for parents and kids, and I've met kids who are seven years old and are having 30 seizures a day.

Camp Oz—which caters to kids ages 9 to 17 who have seizures— is a wonderful place for kids, and I have seen so much there... so much difficulty. I have seen kids who have kits that are with them all the time, with maybe 25 different kinds of medications they take. I've seen parents who go to Colorado to get medical marijuana for their kids.

I have been around parents whose kids have cancer and parents whose kids have epilepsy, and it's the same feeling. You have to ask yourself "Why?" And the parents of these kids have to be the most special people in the world. How would you like to see your child have seizures—I mean violent seizures—30 times a day, some more than that? You know, they will never be able to develop cognitive skills or live normal lives.

I recall painfully having to put our yellow lab down because of the seizures she had. She had always protected me, and even though she had never been trained in that regard, we had a special bond. Rebecca kind of knew when I might be close to having a seizure because Abby would come over and sit down right beside me and look sad. She knew one was coming on. It was amazing how those kinds of bonds form and those connections develop. And I have had those kinds of great connections with people too.

When I see people who don't have the opportunities I've been given, it hurts to know what they face. I have been fortunate to have kind of a simplicity to what I have to deal with compared to others. I feel the same about cancer. I'm not sure why I'm here. I guess God thinks I need to be here to continue my work. But you know I have been given a lot of chances, and so many kids never have. I would trade places with them any day just to see them smile and be able to do what they want to do. Some of these kids can't communicate very well, so I would talk to the parents and watch the tears run down their faces.

There are so many diseases and illnesses that we know a lot about. And there are others that we know little about. Epilepsy is one of those that kind of gets pushed to the back. There is a constant struggle as to what to do. I think some of the things that have happened to me that caught national attention have brought it to the forefront in some ways. But epilepsy to some is like a bad word. That's one of the real negatives, and sometimes seeing people make fun of those with epilepsy, or a disabled person, is tough. And sometimes it's just kids being mean to other kids.

It's because of all this that Rebecca and I and the Epilepsy Foundation have joined together to try to make all the schools in the state of Minnesota "seizure smart." Many grown-ups don't understand epilepsy, and that's hard to watch and understand.

There is not enough done for the disease. It's like it is just put off to the side. With 1 out of 26 people having the disease, it should get more attention. I don't know what information you need other than that.

I mentioned the term *epilepsy* being a "bad word." And I really think it is for some. Mostly this comes from a complete lack of understanding, and I think some who don't understand it are afraid of it. I mean, I have been called a "freak" in an email.

I spoke earlier of the Souhan article and how that not only affected me but people all over the country. Some people think of the word and right away go in their minds to people on the ground flopping around becoming an embarrassment. It is a stigma. The thought is, *Those people are different. They're weird.* It's that kind of thing.

The disease, especially compared to many others, makes me feel very fortunate. That's the way I look at it, anyway. I take the approach that all you have to do is look around and you will find someone much worse off than you are. And as a big-time football coach, I have had the opportunity to see many others much worse off than me. And in the process I hope I have been able to help those people in some way.

I have never felt sorry for myself. Never. Sure, I have had bad days and been depressed about my situation, but I have never gone the route of feeling sorry for myself. I feel sorry for other people. I feel sorry for my family—for Rebecca, for the girls, and for the people who have to watch. I get frustrated because I know Rebecca loves me and my kids love their daddy, and it bothers me what this has done to them.

The caregivers are the ones who take the punishment. The seizure patients don't even know what the hell has happened. They just know they are sore and tired and their thought process is all mixed up. In my situation, I feel sorry for the people who have to deal with me. I feel sorry for my family and my friends, and I feel sorry for the University of Minnesota.

I blame myself. I have always felt that I brought it on myself due to the lack of sleep and lack of taking care of my body. The simple fact is that I married the University of Minnesota. I married Northern Illinois University, Southern Illinois University, and all the others. I was married to football. It's what I did.

Rebecca was always behind me with all my jobs. She has always supported me in everything I have done. When the Minnesota job came up, I can recall saying, "Are you sure you want to do this one? This is going to be really tough. This is going to be like the Southern Illinois job."

Minnesota was going to be different. I know I said it more than once as Rebecca and I discussed it. "This is going to be different. It's going to be tough. It's going to take some years off our lives," I repeated a few times to her, and she said, "Let's roll. We haven't had any regrets. We have done it at all levels, and we can do it here. I'm with you all the way." In the final call that we made, epilepsy was certainly a factor, a consideration, but it was not going to stand in our way.

One of the things I feel is so important for those with epilepsy is being sure you see the right doctor. Be sure you not only see a neurologist but also an epileptologist. This takes nothing away from the outstanding work of neurologists, but it was the epileptologist who really helped me. I didn't even know what that kind of specialized doctor was until I came to Minnesota. And they deal specifically with seizure disorders and epilepsy. People out there with the disease need to know that this is an avenue for them.

The second thing is never to give up. Jim Valvano, former North Carolina State basketball coach, when he was dying of cancer always preached "Never give up." Whether it is your young kid with 30 or 40 seizures a day or a CEO of a major company, the message has to always be to keep moving forward and never give up. And never to give up hope. As bad as it is, always keep hope on the front burner.

The brain is the most difficult thing to treat and understand. There are drugs out there that really help. Some are experimental and are still in the process of getting approved, but we have to keep trying. People talk and think about whether they would ever take their kid and get them medical marijuana, as I mentioned before. Let me tell you, if I'm watching my kid have 30 or 40 seizures a day, you're damn right I'm going to take my kid to Colorado if that's going to help him or her.

Over the years, I have heard a few people higher up make statements about that, and they don't know what they would do if they were in the position of some of these parents. They don't know! They don't know what it's like to see a loved one have a seizure. They don't know what it's like when you come out of a seizure. They don't know what it's like to have the medication affect a person the way it does. People don't know unless they have been there.

The medications are so problematic. I have taken drugs I can't stand because of the effects they have on me. If the medication doesn't work, you have to find something else. Never give up. If the medication isn't working , don't stay on the same damn shit if it's not working. Strides are being made on drugs and on surgeries, so there is hope out there.

When my career coaching football was threatened two and a half years ago because of epilepsy, it was Dr. Smith who enabled me to extend my career. He educated us on the disease and told me what I would have to do if I wanted to have any kind of normal life again.

I don't want to take anything away from the former athletic director at the University of Minnesota, Norwood Teague, who was here, but I think I would still be coaching if I hadn't had to do a lot of things besides coach football. I believe because of what I was asked to do, I had to do much more than most other coaches. This put tremendous pressure on me and took away from the things

I needed to do to stay healthy, such as required sleep, taking care of my body physically, and eating correctly, which are all so important to physical health.

I was involved in fund-raising, making public appearances, and doing much more than I had signed on for. In many respects, because of being in a dysfunctional process, I didn't eat as well. I never got my exercise, which I knew was important. I was tired. The drug I was on screwed me up, and it took my trip out to see Dr. Smith to get me back on track. On game day and also during the week, it was Kammy Powell, my former trainer at Northern Illinois, who took care of me from the epilepsy standpoint. She knew how to handle everything in this regard.

I worked hard at it after Grand Rapids, and for two years I did pretty well. I got my three meals a day and Maddie Hayes, my assistant, made sure I ate when I was supposed to eat. I love Maddie. "Hey, Coach, did you get your lunch today?" she would ask. She took good care of me. I got into a good exercise routine before practice. I went to church before practice, and all this led to success. I sure wished I had kept myself on that track.

What I am saying here is that what I did is sound advice for others regarding what people need to do to keep healthy. And it is not just for people with epilepsy but for all of us. The body has to be fed right, has to be exercised, and has to get enough sleep.

I don't have the answers for kids, because it might be much different as far as routine and other factors, but for adults, it's pretty easy to figure out what leads to good health. For me, when I get tired and run down and am not eating right, it will bring on the seizures. I know that for sure, and the experience I have had with it tells me what I have to do. So the bottom line here is to become educated on what you have to do to keep a healthy mind and body, and then *do it*!

| eight |

I Fired Myself

WHEN I TOOK THE head coaching job at the University of Minnesota in 2011, I never thought it would end the way it did. As much as I enjoyed every single part of the state of Minnesota and the university, it was perhaps the most difficult time of my life.

In the beginning, I was going all over the state and going 110 miles an hour day after day after day. When I came in to take over the job, I found things that had to be corrected and fixed immediately. We were about to lose scholarships because of our academics. We were way behind in the weight room. We were behind in operational money. We were behind in coaches' salaries. We were behind in drawing people to games. We were behind in how people felt about the program. We were in very bad shape! I'm sorry to say it, but it was true.

I was told by people from all over the country, "You are never going to get it done at Minnesota. It's a bad job." Those were the feelings from the outside about the Minnesota football program. It's just the way it was.

I think it was like that because of the culture that was there and had been there for decades. When you look at other schools, it was important for them to be successful on the football field. Football was a huge priority. It wasn't like that at Minnesota.

All the losing was certainly a contributing factor to the negativity because it had been a reality for so long. And it was that way going way back. The love for Golden Gophers football made a change for the worse after some of the great Minnesota teams of the 1960s and 1970s. Minnesota has had some outstanding seasons in the past and won many national championships. We used that in recruiting, and yet it seemed to have been forgotten by many of the fans and longtime Minnesotans.

I don't know, because I wasn't here, but something changed from the 1970s up until now. Things had really slipped dramatically. The last Rose Bowl team was 1961, playing in the 1962 Rose Bowl. That's a few years back! Glen Mason coached at Minnesota for a while from 1997 to 2006, and Glen was an outstanding coach. A lot of people talk about the time Lou Holtz coached there and those great years, but Coach Holtz had a losing record at Minnesota. It was just tough to win there.

So with that history, I came in and tried to change it. It wasn't close to where Glen Mason had left it. Coach Mason, as I said before, was a good football coach. So we had to work our ass off just to get it back to where Coach Mason had it when he left the program.

I was asked one time if I would have taken the job knowing the condition of the program. My answer was "Probably," because I like challenges. Big-time challenges never scared me off. I mean, that's who I am. That's what got me to where I am. If I was asked that now, I would likely say, "No, I want to go somewhere where I don't have to almost kill myself to win."

But it was what it was. I felt the only way to be successful there was to change just about everything about the football program and anything and everything that had any connection to it.

Our staff worked hard together to get the program right. I put pressure on them to do their jobs, and I didn't want to hear excuses.

We had to fix things and fix them in a hurry if we wanted any chance at winning.

It's interesting, because when you take a job as a head football coach, you don't get to really see what you are getting yourself into. What I mean is you don't get to make a visit and walk around much and see anything. And the reason is, there is a lot of secrecy in the process. There has to be. It's just the way it is in our profession. I understand that, so the bottom line is, you really don't know much of anything until you arrive with the job in hand. I saw a little at Southern Illinois, and some of that was in the dark, as I like to kid Paul Kowalczyk, but nothing compared to what I saw once I had taken the job. It was the same at Minnesota.

The indoor facility at Minnesota was the worst I had ever seen in college football. People really have no idea. We won and we recruited there with our players eating in a hallway. We talked about student welfare while our kids were eating in a damn hallway! How do you recruit to that?

Rebecca said many times, "Jerry, if you got a choice and you could stay at the Ritz-Carlton or a one-star hotel for the same price, where would you stay?" I think that's obvious; you would stay at the Ritz-Carlton.

Keeping that in mind, we knew we would not get the five-star athletes out of high school to go there. People used to say to us, "Why aren't you getting the top kids, the five-star players?" Hell, we had no chance to get them. So we had to go after other kids and develop and coach them. Minnesota was a total reconstruction job.

And then you got outside and around the state, and the negativity toward Gophers football was incredible. It was not good anywhere. And on top of that, when I was hired, I was not a big-name football coach to the Minnesota faithful. Most people had never heard of me, so it was a top priority to get out there and tell people I knew what the hell I was doing.

We had to capture the whole state and get them back in it. This is what I was talking about when I mentioned before that I had to marry the job. We had the inside we had to fix and we had the outside to get back on track as well. I knew what was ahead. I knew it wasn't going to be easy. I knew what we were facing, and I hit it full blast and almost killed myself in the process.

There was a lot of blame that focused on the previous coach there, Tim Brewster. Tim had never been a head coach, and I'll tell you, if anyone had come into Minnesota like he did and had never been a head coach, they would not have had a chance either. It wasn't his fault. If I had come in with Tim's background and had never been a head coach, I wouldn't have made it either. Tim Brewster is a good football coach and got a lot of the blame, which was very unfair. He was not responsible for much that went on at the University of Minnesota.

Right away when you get a new football coach, everyone wants to change *right now*, and it's "Let's go to the Rose Bowl!" I knew and said right up front that we were a long way from that happening, and the fact was, we were not even close. Not only did we have to get the culture fixed from the inside with the players, but we had to fix things from the top down at the university.

I had to sell the president, the athletic director, and on down the line that a turnaround could be done, and at the same time not give them false promises. I didn't tell them we were going to the Rose Bowl. I told them we were in deep shit for some time.

The one thing I had going for me from the credibility standpoint was that when I was at Northern Illinois we beat the Gophers. And that went a long way.

So we had to go after all the things we were behind at. People don't understand unless you are the head of a football program or the head of a major company how hard it is to change the inside culture, let alone the outside culture.

Dan O'Brien, who was with the program under Coach Brewster, and I were all over the state. We were up early in the morning and home late at night. And that was in the off-season. The off-season was not supposed to be like that. We went everywhere selling the program.

I told the people, "Hey, you are going to have to give us time. We have issues and we have problems and we cannot change everything overnight. I'm not promising you anything except we are going to get better every year. It's going to be a slow process, and it may take six to seven years to start winning, but you are going to have to trust us."

There was a lot of negativity about that, but at the same time we got a good reception in the places we went because most of the communities couldn't believe the head coach was out doing that. Dan knew the state. He knew where we had to go. He knew the towns and the high school coaches. I went everywhere. I never said no. I never turned down anyone who wanted me to come. It's the reason I am where I am, because it was impossible to keep doing what I was doing.

I think the best thing we did was open practice up to the public. This allowed people to be able to watch us coach. It gave people a chance to see where the program was and to see where it was going. It made some believers in what we were doing. I couldn't sell the public on false hope; I had to sell some blind faith. This took a lot of time and tremendous effort.

I was asked once, "Coach, what was the toughest thing you had to do to begin the process of changing the culture at Minnesota?" I thought for a second and answered, "The toughest thing to change was everything." There was no chance to win without getting everyone on the same page, so it was simple: *everything* had to change. It wouldn't have mattered if the good Lord was coaching there; it all had to change.

We took it slow, but I found out early on that we had great people there who wanted to win. I think there was an appreciation to my approach of not promising things I couldn't deliver on. I didn't tell them we were going to the Rose Bowl immediately. I think some of my personality, being a Midwest guy, helped too.

Every place I went, I gave the same message: "This is not Jerry Kill's football team, it's yours. You are the stockholders in this football team, that's the truth, and it is my job to get you a good football team. And if I can't get you that good football team, then you need to fire my ass." I said that everywhere. I never had a fear of getting fired, never was fired. Eventually, though—and unfortunately—I fired myself.

A lot had to be changed, and it required an unbelievable amount of my time. I had to put it in. And to do that, I had to in the process go through two athletic directors and was on a third on an interim basis. That's three athletic directors in the space of less than five years.

Joel Maturi was the one who hired me, and for sure he rolled the dice. He took a lot of heat about that, no question. I love Joel, and he was a good boss to work for and I will forever be appreciative of him for giving me the opportunity to coach in the Big Ten conference at the University of Minnesota. But Joel told me early on that he didn't know how long he would be there.

I know I pushed Joel hard. He didn't always say yes, but he did his best under some really difficult circumstances. Again, people were on Joel, and he knew a lot of his power as the athletic director had been diminished. As a result he gave me the okay to do what I had to do. If I felt I needed to talk with the president, I had his blessing.

I am one of those guys who, if I felt we needed to get something done, I pushed hard and went after it. I told people, "We are burning daylight here. We need to get this done!" I wasn't afraid; I said what needed to be said. It is the only way I know how to do business. What I said and what I did were not always the most popular things with people. I didn't care. They had to be said and done. I was brought to Minnesota to win football games, and I was going to honor that commitment. And if I had to upset a few people along the way, so be it!

I went to people and asked, "Can you get this done?" I needed to find out who could get what I wanted. Regent Dave Larson was a huge help. He asked me about the problems, and I told him. One of the biggest was the academics. I told him, "We got big problems in this whole area of academics." I told him what we needed. He listened, got up out of his chair, and came back three or four days later with a check for a half million dollars, and said, "Let's get this thing straightened out."

So we were able to get more tutors and more computers, and to get all the kids one of those computers when they came in. Larson gave money to the weight room and other places that were in critical need. I had to count on people, and many came through like Dave Larson had.

I felt like these were all things that *I* had to do. I didn't expect my coaches to get involved in all these things. They had one assignment, and that was to coach football. Just to coach football. I would handle the rest, and it ultimately became too much for anyone to handle.

I turned into a CEO, the head football coach, and a million other things. And then Joel left, so I had to start all over again with the new athletic director. When Norwood came in, he did some good stuff to keep us going and follow up on what Joel had done. I mean, Joel really helped us make a lot of progress.

I had never met Norwood Teague before he came in as the new athletic director. The problem was he had never been close to a football program and really didn't understand our needs. He was more of a basketball guy, and that was a big problem for us. In addition, he came from the outside and didn't know anyone there. That wasn't his fault, but it put extra duties and responsibilities on me to meet with people and get what we needed to be a successful football program.

One of the big problems initially was when we took North Carolina off the schedule. There is a long story to this, and a lot of people were upset about it. I'm the one who took all the heat for the change, but there was more to it than that. A lot that went with it was never made public, and the bottom line was I got blamed.

There was a breakdown in duties and responsibilities at the university, and as a result I had to take on the responsibilities of the football program and many other areas as well. I was involved in fund-raising, speaking all over, and meeting with people, and I was really wearing myself out. With the change in athletic leadership, my responsibilities dramatically increased. Eventually I was able to get Dan O'Brien as an assistant athletic director in charge of football, and that helped considerably.

It seemed like my life at the time never got a break. When other head coaches and their staff were taking time off during certain parts of the summer, my staff and I didn't. There was so much to do; it was unbelievable. And I was wearing myself down.

We ran football camps for kids, and I was at every camp and then was on the road speaking at night. It was too much. It was a process that we had to do, and it finally caught up with me and I simply crashed and burned. A lot of that was my fault. I'm the type of person who never lets up with all that I have to do. I put aside all the things I had been doing for the past couple years to get better health-wise.

Another thing that was going on at the time was my whole contract issue, which was only important to me because it was going to give my coaches a raise. I never cared about me and that damn contract; it was only for the coaches. The contract was a mess. I was promised things that never happened, and it took forever; I think it lingered more than a year. It created more pressure and more frustration. I recall at the time saying to Dan O'Brien, "This whole thing is going to blow up someday, and it's not too far off in the future. I've got good intuition, and this thing is going to blow up."

Things were not good. I was not getting any sleep at night and things in the athletic department were simmering. I felt like things were as bad as they could get for me. I was extending myself beyond even what I had been doing in the past...and then it got even worse.

All the things we were going through on a day-to-day basis were crashing in on me, and the frustration from everything mounted. Little things just became a grind day in and day out, such as going over to the stadium for practice and not having a place to park and then getting a parking ticket. I said before that I am a grinder, but that grind was not what I had signed up for.

Think about it for a minute: The head football coach at the University of Minnesota in the Big Ten conference drives over to the stadium for practice and has no place to park and gets a parking ticket. I mean, it was unbelievable. We weren't allowed to park anywhere, so I remember at times we parked on the sidewalk with recruits in the car. The parking situation was horrible. Can you even imagine that happening at Michigan or Ohio State?

There was one time when Rebecca pulled into my regular parking spot by the office and was sitting in the car and got a ticket. It's like you can't even make this stuff up, but it was happening. Facing all we had to do and then facing the grind of all those ridiculous problems eventually took its toll. It was like we had more difficulties from the inside than we did from the outside around the state.

Eventually I figured some things out as we headed toward fall practice in 2015. Maddie in our office and Adam Clark were doing a great job of keeping things together and watching out for me and my health. And then it all hit the fan when Norwood Teague resigned suddenly in the midst of a sexual harassment investigation.

We had a new interim athletic director in Beth Goetz, who had her hands full with everything that was going on. I like Beth, and we worked well together for the short time I coached under her.

I worked hard to get into a good routine and did my best to take care of myself with the help of others and my family. But as the season was beginning, the simple fact was I was completely worn out. I had been dealing with the whole contract situation as I mentioned, and was really concerned for the assistant coaches and their salaries. And all that just ate at me every day.

I felt like we were going to have a good season because we had built a pretty good foundation over the past few years. But my physical and mental health were concerns for me, and then on top of everything, we had the new sports complex and the $180 million in funding looming out there. There was just so much going on.

One thing I was grateful for in that regard was the help we got from the Big Ten Network, and that was when Teague was still the athletic director. Gerry DiNardo was always talking about how bad things were at Minnesota with regard to our facilities. He used to say we had the worst facilities in the Big Ten, and he asked, "How can kids be eating in the hallway?" So I really compliment him and the Big Ten Network for helping us get those new facilities.

With all that was going on with the fund-raising, we finally got on board with the new facility. And Norwood got on board with it and then helped too. But the fact is Regent Larson came through with a big donation, and that got it on track. And then he also gave a significant donation to the Epilepsy Foundation as well. He was just a very giving guy. He really believed in me and what we were doing and stepped up.

Others stepped to the plate as well. The facilities plan was so important for the future, and that was also a big part of what was wearing me out. As I look back, we had things at Northern Illinois University that we didn't have at Minnesota. It's hard to believe but true. Everybody talked about the bigger stage and the Big Ten, but hell, we were operating like a school in a lesser division.

I mentioned the crashing and burning. Well, it was happening. I was tired. I didn't have much left in me as the season was beginning.

I had been giving everything I had, everything that was left in me. It was the same as I had done everywhere, but at U of M it was much more, and a tougher culture to deal with.

We struggled some in the early games, but that had little effect on me. Football is football, and that's what comes with the territory. It wasn't that. We could have won the TCU game right at the end, but again, that's football. I had been handling things associated with the game my whole career. It was everything else that got to me.

The season became tougher and tougher, and we were having some football issues. The injuries piled up, we got beat by Northwestern and I was trying to do too much. I got more involved in the offense, was trying to rectify the injury problems with figuring out who was going to play, and I was going in earlier, working even harder, and not taking care of myself.

What eventually happened to me was because I got out of that important routine I had been in. I didn't get my walk in during the day. I was missing church. I wasn't sleeping again. I wasn't eating right again, and I was taking everything home with me. I was struggling.

I would get maybe two and a half hours of sleep at night. My mind was racing all the time. It never let up, and then I would get up in the morning tired and start it all over again. That had started at the beginning of the season, and by the time we were several games into it, my life was spinning. I was in serious trouble.

But before I go any further with my condition, I want to make one thing perfectly clear: the University of Minnesota gave me some of the best five years of my life. They provided me with an income status that is unbelievable for a farm kid from Cheney, Kansas. I have met some of the best people I have ever known. My family and I love Minnesota and we love and appreciate what the state has done for us. We made lifelong friends everywhere we went in the wonderful state of Minnesota.

And I will always remember the players and all they did for me, my coaches, the university, and the state of Minnesota. I had the privilege and honor of coaching some great kids at Minnesota. And with these kids we had some big wins—over Michigan, Nebraska, Penn State, and quite a few others. We went to a major bowl game for the first time in 50-some years and increased the team's overall grade point average to a 3.0 seven semesters in a row. These were all major program accomplishments that will greatly benefit the future of Gophers football. The program started to turn, and I believe it will keep the turn going and that good things are ahead for the University of Minnesota.

It is important to me that I not paint the story here in the wrong way. Each job has its challenges, and I chose to do what I was doing. I could have stepped back and said, "I'm not going to do this." But I didn't. It was my choice, and I am not blaming anybody for what eventually occurred. I love the university. I love the state of Minnesota, the people who live there, and all my players. There is not a place in the state where they don't say to me, "Hey, Coach, we appreciate everything you've done." And I appreciate everything that was done for me. I cannot say that strongly enough.

I told Rebecca, "We have been in a lot of great places and we have reached a lot of people, but I don't know if we ever developed friendships with the community, the players, the student body, and the university like we have here." We wish we could have stayed and remained a part of the community and the university.

I have never been called Jerry by the students like I was in Minnesota. The whole Jerrysota tribute is pretty damn humbling. I never experienced anything like that before. It is as good as any place we have ever been. We will have friends there forever. It was a great ride.

My connection with the students and the band was unbelievable. When I would walk out on the field and the band and the students would yell the Jerrysota thing, you just have no idea of the effect of something like that on a person. I have been so impressed with the enthusiasm at the games and the attendance. And people will tell you this is a tough place to come and play, and it didn't used to be that way.

I love people and I am a loyalty sucker. I'm loyal to people who have worked with me and whom I have been with over the years. I'm loyal to the fans and the state. And having said that, I feel like I let everyone down when I came forward and said, "I can't do it anymore." And I feel bad about that.

As the 2015 season progressed, it seemed like I had more and more to do and was getting less and less sleep. But as I said, this had been coming from way back in the summer. I recall telling Rebecca one day, "Man, it seems like I am in a battle every single day. I am just wore out." The fun hadn't left me quite yet, because of the players. I have always loved my players. I absolutely loved all my players, and I would do anything I could to help them. They are the ones who win games. I have always had a great relationship with my players. I loved being around them and had a good time with them.

But then the grind of the season hit me harder than ever before. I had always said when the grind wasn't fun anymore, I was going to be done. When coaching football became a job, then it was time. And it had started to become a job for me, and it was becoming that because I had let it become that.

All my bad habits had come back. I wanted to do it all and please the state of Minnesota. I wanted to win for the state and the kids, not for me.

If I had never gone to Minnesota, I had a great career, winning everywhere I had been. But at U of M I wanted to win so badly for the fans. It had been years since they knew anything about winning.

So there we were. We were in the middle of our bye week, and I had had a couple situations at night, seizures I mean, and Rebecca was sitting up all night watching me. And I was thinking, *This is no way to live. We can't keep doing this.* I said, "What the hell am I doing?" We had reached Monday after the bye week before the Michigan game, and I was in big trouble.

So I went and talked with a Catholic priest and told him what I was going through. I talked to former coach Bobby Ross because I knew he had gone through some bad times and left in the middle of a season when he was coaching the Detroit Lions. He had crashed and burned like me. I talked to my friends Carl Mauck and Roger Lipe to tell them where I was at, and it all helped me. They all helped me. And then I called Dr. Brien Smith.

Dr. Smith really set me straight. He said, "Hey, you have had a great career. You have got your family and you've got football." And he said, "You know, it might be time to leave. It might be the time to make that decision to leave."

And then I couldn't make the decision. And he would call me and ask, "Did you make it yet?" And I told him, "I just can't do it." And he said to me, "You understand what's going to go on." And in the past I had never listened to a doctor, but I trusted Dr. Smith.

Rebecca didn't know for sure what to tell me. My kids didn't know. We all loved football, and it was a major part of our lives. I'm pretty sure the thinking was that I couldn't live without football. There were all kinds of mixed emotions. The kids loved football, but they and Rebecca loved me and wanted me to be around. Most people don't understand that you can die from epilepsy.

Krystal had been on the sideline with me for years. How was this going to affect her? And Rebecca and Tasha, what about them? Rebecca had been involved in everything at Minnesota more than anywhere else we'd lived.

So I decided I was going to give it another try. I went to practice on Tuesday, and the game plan was all ready and we were ready to go for the Michigan game on Saturday. I said, "I am going to give this one more shot. I know I can do this." But as much as I wanted to do it, I couldn't.

I wasn't coaching out there the way I wanted to coach. I was on medications, making all these adjustments to my life, and the fact was, I wasn't the same Jerry Kill. And that tore me up. I wasn't doing what I do out there on the field; it wasn't me. I could have just gone over and sat in a golf cart or just stood there and watched, but that's not me. It's not who I am.

I could have just gone through the motions and taken home $8 million the next four years. It would have been easy. But I stood out there and said to myself, "I'm cheating the game! I'm cheating the university, the state of Minnesota, and the players." I was telling them out on the field to give 100 percent while I wasn't doing the same. I wasn't coaching. I wasn't involved like I should have been. It was my attitude, my enthusiasm; the fire wasn't there. You can talk to anybody who knows me and they will say, "That Jerry Kill is one fiery SOB!" I mean if the quarterback messed up, I was on his ass. I was coaching. Usually I was everywhere, but not on that day.

It wasn't that it was all that day either. I didn't just walk out on the practice field that Tuesday and lose it. It was gradual, but it was there at that point, and I knew it. My original thought was I would call it quits that previous weekend, but I just couldn't do it. I could not pull the trigger.

I honestly thought that Tuesday that I could make it. I told myself over and over, "I'm gonna be all right. I can do this." When practice ended, I met former All-American player Bob Stein, who brought a young man by the name of Jon Lavalier, who had epilepsy, out to meet me. I had a great visit with Jon and then walked off the field and through the indoor practice field, and I was done.

I went up to my office and closed the door and cried. I thought about everything. I know this for sure: In these tough times, God doesn't come down and tell you what to do. He just gives you subtle hints along the way. I thought about the finances and what was going to happen with that.

And then I recalled something that had been with me a long time, which was, "Hey, count on your health instead of your wealth and count on God instead of yourself." So I said, "I'm going to walk away from $8 million and I don't care. I'm not coaching the way I want to and I'm not having fun."

I knew it was over. There was not a doubt in my mind. There was no rethinking it; it was final. It was just like when I married Rebecca. I knew it was the right thing to do. I went home and worried about the coaches. Back at my office the coaches were also on my mind. *What is going to happen to them?* I wondered. I had to get it set for them so they would all be okay.

I felt I could get Tracy situated to take my place and that would help all the assistants. Dan O'Brien was aware of what I was doing most of the way, but essentially no one else outside my family knew.

I told Rebecca when I got home. I said, "I'm done. Do you support me?" And she said, "I love you and I'm with you." So I called the girls and they cried, and then I called my brother and told him. With Mom, I waited a long time and finally called her about 9:00 that evening and said, "Mom, I'm done. I can't do it the way I want to anymore." She said, "I love you and I got your back." It was the same as my brother had told me.

I told Dan to set up a meeting with the coaches at 6:30 AM and then the players at 7:15 AM. I think our quarterback, Mitch Leidner, knew something was up, because we had not met at that time all year.

Other than losing my dad, that was the toughest moment of my life. I didn't want a press conference, but Dan talked me into it, and it was a good thing to have held it. I'm glad I listened to him.

First I met with the coaches, and they were in shock. I walked in with tears in my eyes and told them I was done. I said, "I'm not doing my job the way I want to do it. I feel I am hurting the team, and I think it's time to turn it over to a bunch of young guys who I have raised, and it will all work out. Trust me; I have it all worked out."

No one said a word. Guys' heads were down. Some tears came down. I told them I loved them. I told them not to worry. I had never let them down, and it was going to be all right. And I left and went to my office.

Rebecca and Krystal came into my office, and then I will never forget when Brian Anderson, one of my coaches who had been with me for a long time, came into my office, and he was crying. He put his arm around me and said, "Coach, you're like my dad." I never knew he felt that way. Others came in, and some couldn't come in.

And then there was the players meeting. I think some of the players felt it was their fault because a few practices before that I was mad and had told them after the practice that it wasn't worth a shit. And I told them, "If I can't get you motivated to play, then why in the hell should I be coaching you?" So they thought maybe that was why I quit.

I made sure they knew that wasn't the reason. I told them what was going on and that I had to take care of my family. I told them I had been taking care of everyone else in my life and I wasn't going to keep going the same way. I told them if they ever needed anything, I would be there for them. I was in kind of a fog, but I got through it. No one said a word, and I went right from there to the press conference.

I walked in and really don't know to this day what I said. I do remember saying that a part of me died and is still dead. A part of me is still out there on that field. I left the press conference thinking, *I got it done.*

I went to my office, and Mitch Leidner walked in and said, "Coach, I don't want you to leave." We talked and talked, and he left. And then it was over. And I walked out of my office for the last time.

| nine |

Life After Football

IT'S THE FIRST TIME in more than 30 years that I haven't been connected to football. I don't have a team to coach. I'm not the players' head coach, and I'm not the boss. I don't have a football office to go to every day. You know, I have been doing a lot of soul searching, and I have faith that this will all get figured out. It was pretty tough walking out of there my last day at the University of Minnesota. The first week and a half I was pretty worn out. I was really tired, so I didn't do a whole lot.

The tribute I got at the Michigan game the week I retired was really nice. I got to see all the fans, and being around the players was in some respects heartbreaking for me. I still stay close to the Gophers, but I went into rehab. As soon as I felt better and could get around some, we went to Florida and walked the beach. We walked anywhere between 6 and 10 miles a day and ate right; I ate a lot of fish and mostly took care of myself.

I know there have been many things I have done that did not help my health situation. All I did for the most part was put a Band-Aid on it, so it was good to get away, and being in the Sunshine State was good for me. We spent a lot of time in Siesta

Key, near Sarasota, and just tried to relax, which is difficult for me to do.

This gave me a lot of time to think. I was really surprised so many people contacted me about the future. I heard from many who said, "Hey, you can help us out when you are ready," so that was really nice. And then Rebecca and I got to talk a lot. We had been with people and different places for a long time, and we wondered what the future held for us. We just kind of put it in God's hands. Who knows what is going to happen down the road? We have a lot of faith and we will just wait and see.

We got to think a lot about old memories and old times, and it was good. Mentally, when you have done something for as long as I have, it's very hard to leave it. At first, I was not going to watch a game, but then I did and I got back into it. It's hard for me to really get away from the game. I did have the opportunity to keep in touch with some of my players and the coaches, so that made it easier for me.

Maddie in the football office was able to keep everything for me—cards and things from all the people who sent me stuff. I even heard from one of the Supreme Court justices, Clarence Thomas, so that was pretty neat. A lot of people have reached out to me.

I have been fortunate to keep in contact with a lot of people, so in some ways it's not like I left the game, only the coaching part of it. I checked in with Tracy Claeys a few times a week during the season, but mainly I kept in touch with the support staff. Our administrative assistants like Maddie, Jenna, Adam Clark, Jeff Jones, and Kammy Powell, who had been our trainer at Northern Illinois, were all very supportive. Those contacts were good for me and kept my spirits up.

I went to the Wisconsin game and the bowl game, and that helped keep my connections, but to be honest, it has been very difficult for me. When you care for something and have done something as long as I have done it, it's tough to leave. You don't just walk away and say, "Okay, I'm ready to go." As time goes by, I know I'm getting better. I watched the national championship game, and it was a great game.

The one thing I have enjoyed doing, because for the first time in 30-some years I have the time now, is to reflect back over the years to think about my favorite part of football: the players and the great teams I have coached.

It's great to think about the past, but putting it down on paper is difficult, because I don't want to leave anyone out. There were so many great players, tough players, talented players, and just good people. Getting to know these kids was the best part for me. There is no doubt I have always had great passion and love for my players, and for me they were the most special part of the game.

I can look at some of the players and know that so many had a personality just like mine. You know, give it all you got, 110 percent all the time, never give up, all those things. I coached a lot of tough guys, and I brought some of those guys with me into the coaching profession. I found so many who wanted to win like me, and as a result we fit together well.

As I look back I recall so many tough guys and great leaders. In order to win, you have to have great leadership, and I had those kinds of players everywhere I have been. It's the same in business; you have to have great leadership in order to succeed. I was fortunate to have great quarterbacks on my teams who were also great leaders, and that's why we won.

My quarterbacks were blessed with great personal qualities and skills, and they blessed our teams with that leadership. It followed me to every stop. I have had players who took charge as quarterbacks and gave it everything they had, and it made the teams great.

Take my last stop at Minnesota—and again, I don't want to leave anyone out, because these guys are all so important to me, but I'll just mention Mitch Leidner as an example of toughness and leadership. The kid had a torn MCL, three broken toes, and a knockdown shoulder…I mean, the guy was unbelievable. He was one tough kid, and I'd run through a brick wall for him.

When you talk about leadership, toughness is in the job description. You have to be able to come forward, and this won't make you the most popular guy all the time. Our leaders took no crap from anyone. They stepped up and led the team. And all they cared about was winning.

My coaching didn't just find leaders and toughness in the quarterback roles but all over. I have had some great players, tough guys, and leaders at all the positions over the years. Great linemen, linebackers, tight ends, running backs, defensive ends, defensive backs, special teams players…I had them all. If I started listing them on each team, the list would be endless.

I saw these kids stand out right away in practice, the first time I saw them on the field. And you know why? Because they took charge. Right away they took charge and stood out. They were tough—I mean tough players. Most of them never went into the training room unless they had something broken or something like that. They stayed out of the training room because they wanted to play. Football was important to them. I've had kids who never missed a game and never went to the training room.

I mentioned some of my quarterbacks over the years being great leaders. I never had to ask one of my quarterbacks to come in and get extra work. Never. That's a sign of someone who wants to do more. I was that way. I wanted to play. I saw my dad break his foot, as I mentioned, and never go to the doctor. My dad was a tough guy. I mean that's the way we were brought up, and I played the game that way. I wanted my players to play the game that way too, and they did.

I recall one summer I hurt my back baling hay. When I came back to fall camp I was told I probably shouldn't play. Hell, this was my senior year in college and there was no way I wasn't going to play.

I've never understood when you are playing a big game how you can stay off the field. I know with the big games that I have been in, I would honestly cut my right toe off if it's what I had to do to play. That's how much passion and respect I have for the game. "Go ahead, put my arm in a sling; I'll be out there. Broken bone, suit me up. I'm ready to go." It's the way it is, and I coached many like that.

I think any time you have a good football team, it reflects on the coach and the staff, and vice versa. The players look up to the coaching staff, and if you have coaches who are tough and disciplined and who want to win, you'll win.

I have had players who were great players for me and went on to be high draft choices and play in the National Football League, some for many years. These were tough guys, with big-time motors inside them that never shut down, and I really enjoyed watching them play. I never had the size or physical ability, but I did have that passion for the game and the motor that never shut down. And I have coaches like that who have been with me for many years, some more than 20 seasons. And the players see that and watch that, and it rubs off on them.

I have had some players who were so blessed with physical ability and passion for the game, mixed with a little anger, that it wasn't coaching; all we had to do was watch them play and enjoy it.

All our teams had the kinds of players I have been mentioning. We had great players with tremendous leadership and passion. And that's why we won every place we went.

I felt like I was going to be at Minnesota for a long time. I had rebuilt programs with my coaching staff over the years and I thought Minnesota might be my last stop. I mean, we were finally going to get the facilities we needed. Just after I left they put a shovel in the ground to begin what we had fought for, for so long. There were so many people who stepped up to the plate and delivered.

Outside football, which was my second marriage for three decades, I did not have a lot of other interests besides being with my family. When I did get a short vacation or some time away, I would spend it with Rebecca and the kids. When Krystal and Tasha were younger, they were good athletes and I traveled around and watched them play their games. The bottom line for me had been football and family. That's what I did, and I'm fortunate because Rebecca and my kids love football too, so it's been a great fit for all of us. Football and family—it sure has a nice ring to it.

As I look back, with the programs I took over, there just wasn't much off-time. We had to work to make the turnaround, and it wasn't easy. As a result, my interests outside football and family have been limited. Maybe now, my life will slow down some and I can find the time for more interests. Having said that, though, I don't think I have missed anything, because I have a huge family that keeps me busy and always will. What I mean is, in addition to my own family, I have my football family, composed of the hundreds of kids I have coached and the coaches I have been with, and I would do anything for any one of them.

I'm not a golfer, a crossword puzzle guy, or big on television, but I do like to read. I like Navy SEAL stuff, football stuff, and autobiographies. I like to read about coaches and how they do things and why, but that's about it.

I also really enjoy speaking and have done a lot of it. I enjoy the teaching aspects of the game as well. As far as things like puzzles and stuff, my mind never shuts down enough to get involved in things like that. My mind is moving all the time. No matter what I try to do to enjoy myself away from the game, my mind always takes me back. That's been my problem. I never have been able to get away and relax. I'm wired differently. That's what the doctor told me, and I guess that has been a big contributor to all my health problems.

I think now I may have a chance to really relax and get a chance to do some things I haven't been able to do before. We just went through a major move, and it's the first time in all the moving we have done that I have been around to do it with my wife. And we had no major altercations, so that's pretty good.

As I said, since I left coaching I have had the opportunity to do some things I never had the time to do before. I got to spend time this year with my whole family at Christmas, and that was just great. I got to open gifts together this year with my family and with Rebecca's family, and it was a good time. I really enjoyed it, and spending time with my mom this year was special too. I never got to do that before, because we were always in a bowl game or some kind of playoff game.

I have for the first time in a long time had the luxury of taking care of myself, eating right, getting my exercise in, and basically just relaxing. And I have enjoyed it.

I have even taken the time to write this book. I wanted to reach out to people to tell them that not everything was perfect in Jerry Kill's life. I want people to know that just because I love the game, it's no easy path to success.

I got in the game for the right reasons. I love kids and I love the players, and I wanted to coach. I just wanted to tell my story but at the same time educate people on how we ran programs and how coaching is similar to running a business.

I wanted to talk about epilepsy and cancer from the medical side. I wanted this book to be different. I didn't want it to be just about football but to cover so much more in life. I wanted this to be a well-rounded book that could touch a lot of people's lives, from football fans to businesspeople to cancer and epilepsy patients… and everyone in between.

Since I retired, things have been going great for Rebecca and me. I have been keeping really busy. We have traveled back to my hometown and to several places where I coached. I have also been doing a lot of speaking at various places around the country, including corporate groups, medical organizations, and for the Chicago Bears and the National Football League.

I have also been invited by coaches to watch and evaluate practices at Miami of Ohio, TCU, and Minnesota, and spoke at coaching clinics at Notre Dame and North Dakota State, while also observing their practices. In addition, I have been spending a lot of time with my former quarterback, who is the head coach at Southern Illinois University, and his football team, watching and evaluating. Coach Nick Hill, at only 30 years of age, is doing a great job in the lead role for the Salukis. I am having a real blast and absolutely loving the speaking engagements and being involved in the game.

When I look at my life, I can tell you that the only thing that is really important to me is to somehow make a difference in others' lives. At the end of the day, what you do for your family and for others is all that counts. I was once told by one of my staff, Terry Szucs, "Coach, they aren't going to put your wins and losses on your tombstone. What's going to be on there is how you treated people and what you did for others."

If someone asked me what I would want my legacy to be, I would want people to say, "He gave everything he had to everyone he ever worked for and everybody he ever met, and he always had their back. The guy did it the right way. He's a good guy. He gave everything he had to the game, treated people with respect, and had a lot to say about a lot of things; and he cared. He cared about people." That's what I would want them to say.

| ten |

Loving the Game

I LOVE ALL SPORTS, REALLY. In high school I played every sport but I wanted to play in college and didn't have the ability to go to a big school. I knew the only shot I had was to play football at a smaller school. I got into college at Southwestern and played for Coach Franchione. I was not a great talent, but I studied football and worked very hard at learning the game.

I watched a lot of film and became kind of like a coach. I enjoyed that process very much, and then when I got a chance to volunteer and help out my last semester there, I just said, "You know, I love being around kids. I love the strategy. I love the team part of the game." I mean, football is the ultimate team game, and you don't see that as much in other sports.

I learned so much from the game when I played. And then over all the years I coached, I have learned so much more. It's a game where you have to rely on somebody else. You cannot do it on your own. The relationships you build are special because it is a big team game. Football has you working with all of your teammates, and there is so much communication. It's just different than other sports.

There are basic fundamentals and life lessons that you learn from the game of football. The camaraderie you get from football is special, and it is very similar to what life is all about. The game often teaches you what you can't learn in the classroom.

Something that is really important in football or any game is respect for the game. Respect for the game is not about what you are doing for the game; it is what the game is doing for you. How you act while you are playing the game is important, as is playing by the rules. The game is a team game, not an "I" game. Respecting the game is about playing the game the way it is supposed to be played and not having the game be about you. The "me" mentality is one drastic way the game has changed.

Over the years the game has changed in a lot of ways, though. Back when I was playing, we didn't really have any trainers. I mean, I did the taping sometimes. One of the big things that has changed is the whole drinking water thing. I remember when players never drank water. It was a sign of weakness if you drank water. We had salt tablets that we would swallow, and that was it. You might get one water break during a practice, but you didn't dare ever ask for any water.

Another big change is the whole knee issue. A torn ACL back in my day was referred to as a sprained knee. The way players train is different too. But one of the biggest changes has been in attitudes. Back in the day I think there was more of a team-oriented approach. Today everything is such a big business that it brings about some of the self-entitlement that we never had before. The team concept is missing some.

The strategies of the game have changed as well; many don't even resemble those of the past. Everyone seems to throw the football now, and because of the size and speed of today's players, concussions from big hits are threatening the game.

Concussions are one of those things, like anything else, that the more awareness there is of something, the more attention it gets. Because of this attention today, the game of football is under a microscope.

Concussions are a big issue in soccer and hockey too. Many sports are being forced to take a hard look at themselves. Athletes in general are becoming bigger, stronger, and faster, and therefore sports are becoming more violent. The collisions are harder, more brutal, and when you put all this together, the injuries are going to become more frequent and more serious in nature.

I think football is trying to do everything it can to make the game safer at all levels. The basic fundamentals of tackling are being taught differently in an attempt to keep people healthy. I think all you can do is continue to bring awareness to the game and do everything you can to make sure the players are safe.

When you think about it, football used to be played with leather helmets. And when it was, you know players didn't go in there and throw their heads into the tackles the way they sometimes do today. We have to find more ways to keep players safe by teaching proper playing methods that reduce the risks. We can't allow the more protective helmets to cause more reckless play because they make the head safer. And we can't allow players to use the safer helmets, in effect, as weapons on the field.

The image out there for much of the public is that football is a game that is becoming too dangerous to play. I'm particularly worried about the college game. With the concussion issue and the general violence of the game, many parents—including some current and former NFL players—won't let their kids play football. I think there have to be some rule adjustments, because the game is being threatened.

But I see another side too. While it may be unpopular, I am one of those old-school people who believes when it is your time for something to happen, it happens.

There are a lot of sports besides football that can result in serious injury. You can get hit in the face with a baseball, break an arm or leg in basketball, break bones and suffer catastrophic injury skiing, get a puck in the face in hockey, and so on. All sports come with injury potential, but do the risks take away from the incredible rewards that go with sports? Absolutely not, in my opinion.

I just look back on my life and those that I have been around in sports, especially football, and know the tremendous rewards, life lessons, and other benefits far outweigh the potential risks.

I can give example after example over my three decades in football of kids whose lives changed because of the game. Every year I have been coaching, I have seen kids whose lives have been saved because of football. It's all some of these kids have. We have to do what we can to keep the game alive, and that starts with continued education about the game's risks and ways to prevent them.

Another issue at the forefront of modern football is that of paying college players. I think kids should be supplemented in the summer. The way college football is structured today, players don't get summer jobs because of the training schedule in place as they prepare for the season.

When I was going to school, I was able to work because there was not so much structure in place for such things as running and weight lifting. To me, college football ought to be treated like a job in the summer. Take into consideration what a player might earn at a summer job, and pay them accordingly for their participation in the football program. Summer wages would be a great help to many of the kids. There are players who come into college programs with literally nothing. They don't have any money, their parents don't have any money, and they struggle every day just to survive. I have picked up kids from the airport, and all they have with them is one small bag. I mean that's it, one bag and that's all they have. I have seen it many times. They get off the plane, one bag in hand, and it's, "Coach, I'm ready to go." It's sad; they don't have nothing.

Being a football coach is so much more than the game and what happens on Saturday. Having said that, I confess that I love

Some said "Jerry who?" But I was ready to tackle my next challenge as the head coach at Minnesota.

Being the coach has its perks. Here I am with former Gophers star Jim Carter (left) and the great Carl Mauck (right).

A coach is only as good as his staff, and mine was outstanding.

Celebrating taking home the Little Brown Jug with Cedric Thompson.

Carrying on a tradition of charity work at Minnesota. At this game, the Gophers cheerleaders pose with Billy Drash, a remarkable young man living with epilepsy, who we supported through the Coach Kill Fund.

When I first met Mia Gerold, she was fighting cancer. Over the years we've formed a great friendship, and I'm happy to say that her cancer is today in remission.

Player outreach has always important to me. Here the Gophers visit with a young fan during a community event.

I'm so proud of the work that has been and continues to be done at Camp Oz.

I met Maja Nord many years ago and was deeply affected by her story of struggling with epilepsy. Our family continues our friendship with her today.

We've put a lot of emphasis into education, going to schools to teach about epilepsy.

Deb Hadley is doing great work every day. She lost her daughter, Kaylie, at age 24 to Sudden Unexpected Death From Epilepsy (SUDEp) and her son, Tyler, at age 17 to another tragedy. Here we are together at their 2015 memorial 5K.

Raising money—and awareness—for epilepsy research and treatments.

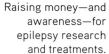

Right: I was overwhelmed by the outpouring of support from the team, university, and community.

Below: And I was deeply honored to raise the banner of "Jerrysota" that the UM student body conferred upon me.

Stepping down was difficult, but I cherish those years I spent in Minnesota.

My mother (center) and Rebecca are two of the strongest women I know.

And my brother, Frank, is a constant source of inspiration and support. We complement each other so well.

Tasha's wedding day was special for all of us.

There is nothing in the world so important to me as my family. I love Rebecca and my girls, Krystal and Tasha, so very much.

winning! I love competing. And when we lost, it was like dying. However, winning means many things. You want to win as many football games as you can, but in the end, I don't believe you will be judged on how many football games you won. You are judged on how these kids turn out 5, 10 years down the road. That's when you hear about it the most.

Did you do your job in the four or five years those kids were with you? Did you teach those kids proper values, teach them all the things they were going to see and be faced with in life? Did you teach them to handle adversity, and did you make them better people? And the only way you can find all this out is to catch up with them 5 to 10 years down the road. *Finding out that you did your job with these kids is the win that counts! That's the big win!*

I didn't get into this business for the love of money but for the love of kids. I got into it to coach them, teach them life's lessons, help them out, and be there for them. This is what I am going to miss the most about coaching. It's what drove me and motivated me every day.

Hell, I'm the only guy in the world who walked away from $8 million in the rest of my contract at Minnesota because I didn't feel like I was giving the kids what they needed. I would not cheat the kids or the game by not giving my players everything I had. So I stepped away. I wanted to be a second dad to them, but I just couldn't do it the way I had in the past anymore.

I worry about my players when they're with me and after they leave. It concerns me when some leave for the NFL too early. In basketball a kid can go pro after one year in college. In football, it's a couple years longer, and may be okay, but I still worry about it. For some it's the right thing, but for others it is not. They may not be mature enough to handle the money, the competition, and all the pressures that can go with it. So it's best to sort it all out for each individual kid. I feel like maturity-wise, kids should play three full years of college football first, and then if they are ready, let them go to the NFL. I think we let them go too early sometimes.

As I mentioned, a lot of the kids are not prepared to handle their money. Bart Scott, as I mentioned earlier, played for me at Southern Illinois. He took care of his money and is out speaking now about how to do it. He was on the ESPN show *30 for 30* that talked about players who had gone broke. He has the right perspective.

I can tell you that every single player I know who left early missed playing college football. Even guys who have done well and made the pro team, they will tell you they missed college football.

Professional football is a tough, hardcore business. College is tough too, but it's still a game for young people. Many areas—even the locker rooms—are different in the professional ranks. Not to mention those jobs are not guaranteed. A kid could leave college for the pros and then be out of professional football real quick; you have to watch out for that happening.

Leaving a school to go somewhere else is also a big deal for coaches, and it can be very difficult. I was one of them. When I left jobs to take another one, it was really tough. I referenced previously how difficult it was at Northern Illinois. We played in a championship game, and the next day Minnesota flew down and talked to me about their head coaching job. Then on Sunday we had our banquet and I accepted the Minnesota job and flew out the next day.

And during all that, the word that I was leaving leaked out, and it was one of the most disappointing moments of my life. It was terrible. And I couldn't do anything about it. I couldn't do one damn thing about it unless I turned down the job. It hurt kids. I couldn't even coach in our team's bowl game, and it was awful.

The media makes it hard. I mean, you cannot go to a place and walk around the campus, because if a reporter or photographer sees you, your presence on that campus will be leaked. Most of the time meetings about jobs take place at a neutral site. You can't take a chance on being seen and having the word leak out, like what happened to me when I left Northern Illinois. When news of my departure leaked, the players were upset, recruits were upset, coaches were upset; I mean, it was a mess. But kids are resilient, and I still keep in contact with many of my former Northern Illinois players and community friends. Others told me at the time and later on that they would have done the same thing if in my position.

I'm not sure exactly what the answer is to prevent sudden departures and the damaged feelings that accompany them. At one time I thought maybe the deal is that colleges ought to wait until recruiting is over after the bowl games before making job offers. Well, I changed my mind because that will still injure those who you just recruited. I mean, hell, you have just recruited these kids, and then you leave before they even arrive? So it's a hard question to answer, it really is, and I'm just not sure what the solution is.

I mentioned rules earlier, but I want to hit it a little harder here. There are rule changes in place that I think have been good and have made the game of college football safer, such as tackling technique. However, two of the most dangerous plays for football players are the point after touchdown and field goal. The offensive lineman has to sit in there and protect, and the defensive lineman can just tee off on them. I mean, they can do almost anything they want to do to the poor offensive guy who has to just sit there. The offensive linemen can't back up and protect themselves, and sometimes they have to take a hit from up to three players on defense. They can get the living crap kicked out of them. No one wants to be the PAT/field goal team. I mean, what are we supposed to tell those guys?

That's a rule I would change right away. Maybe there should be a rule where the only rush should come from the outside, and no rushing the kicker and holder from the inside. It's a very dangerous play, and I could never understand why it didn't cause a rule change. I mean, we're very concerned about one-on-one plays, but here we have three-on-one in some instances, and we don't do anything about it. It's not right and should be looked at carefully for changes to protect players. I like the NFL's rule for extra points, which brought the line for the kicker back. It has made a difference in the game and brought the two-point conversion more to the front.

I also like the college overtime rule and how that has made the game more interesting. It seems to be fair to both teams and then makes it even more interesting at the point where a team has to go for the two points. It's a good rule.

I want to talk about the speed of the game for a minute too. Instant replay is good, because it ensures the call on the field is right, but it takes too long. We are at the point of four-hour games, and that is too damn long! I think they are working on ways to move it along faster, but it is a problem. Another thing that could be changed that would speed up the overall length of games is the rule that stops the clock after every first down, but that has been in for so long it is not likely to change.

The biggest thing for me is to look at things that include making the game safer. One thing that the higher-ups are looking at is the kickoff and kick returns components to the game. This would be a major change, but would keep some of the tremendous contact that comes with the kickoff from occurring. Most people close to the game agree with this and I think it would have a significant impact on concussions.

But even though there are some rules I would change, I love the game of football! At this point I don't know what my future will be. I have had a lot of calls to stay in the game, but I'm not sure at this point what I am going to do. A lot of me died the day I walked off the field for the last time. I knew I was not going to be able to do it my way anymore and that it was time. I think taking the time off will really help me from a health standpoint. It will enable me to get my health in order and not just keep putting Band-Aids on over and over again.

I don't blame anybody for what happened to me health-wise. I take full responsibility. I brought it all on myself, I really did. I tried to do too much. I never said no to anybody. I did whatever I was asked to do, and that's what caused all the problems. If I was supposed to do the job of the athletic director, it was always, "Okay, what do I do?" I think if I had learned how to say no, I would still be coaching.

Like I said, I don't know what I am going to do down the road, but I do know that somehow I will be a part of the game. Maybe it will be working with high school kids, working with another coach somewhere, or being a position coach down the road…I'm just not sure. I would even consider some time of administrative work connected to athletics. Or maybe I will go in a different direction and do something I have never done before. But football will always be in my life somewhere. The game has been too good to me, and I feel like I owe too much to the game. I know the future will be different for me from the way I operated in the past. I hope so, anyway.

I love the game of football. And coming with that love of the game comes what I believe is a responsibility of the coaches. The fact is coaches are role models and should not put themselves in a position where the most important thing is chasing the almighty dollar bill. Money has done a lot to the game, and most of it is not for the best.

The camaraderie that existed when I got into the coaching profession more than 30 years back is missing to some extent today. I can remember when several of us from various teams would be out heavily recruiting some kid and then that evening all be in the same bar or restaurant talking football. There was still competition, but the relationships the coaches developed were really special. This still happens some, but the money involved is so incredible now that it will never be quite the same.

Of course, you still have coaches that love coaching the game and love the kids and are in it for the players. But I also think today you have a lot of coaches who are in it for the money; they're chasing paper. I have watched that change happening over the years.

I look back at when John Mackovic got the job at Texas, and that's when I think it all started. I believe Texas paid their assistants all kinds of money, and there it all went. I mean, you now have offensive and defensive coordinators in college ball making more than a million dollars a year. And let me tell you, with the pressures that go with the game in today's environment, they earn every penny. It was never that way in the old days.

Today coaches have a very small window in which to win. Some are fired after three years, whereas in the past a coach had a lot more time to turn a program from a losing one to a winning one.

As I look back, it seems like it used to be just about playing ball and coaching ball. None of us cared about what we made or what the coaches over there made. It was what we did, and we loved every part of it. "Hell, $40,000 a year, that's a hell of a living. Let's go coach some ball!"

Now everybody is moving from one staff to another and to this place and that place. It's nuts! I have a friend who was at one place making $500,000 a year and went somewhere else for $600,000. The money is a big part of it.

I can't complain about the money. There's no doubt it has made my life better, but I have never forgotten where I came from. Money does strange things to people, it really does. And I think when someone makes too much of it, there is no doubt it can change that person, and not necessarily for the good. Some people do forget where they came from in some way, shape, or form.

With me, I'm kind of that old-school type of guy. I always remember my past and my commitment and loyalty to the game and to my staff and colleagues. We knew how to coach and at the same time take care of each other. And all this kind of stuff has changed a bunch, and it's too bad, because it's not good for the game.

I think it's only the coaches who can get this turned around and get what's important back to the forefront. The coaches have got to come together and change the damn thing. Administrators today don't really have a true understanding of the game unless they played it, so it's got to be the coaches. It's the strongest union that we have. It's going to be damn tough to change these attitudes and for sure the money involved. But it's important.

In addition, coaches have a strong chance to be role models for our players. If you are telling the kids not to do certain things and then you are out doing them, well, I don't understand that. I mean, there is nothing wrong with going out and having a beer, but the responsibility we have as coaches is important. And there is no better example than the one you set by your own behavior.

We see coaches doing all kinds of things and getting released from their teams for doing this or doing that, and you just step back and say, "What the hell is wrong with them?" The coaches in today's game have a huge responsibility to kids, maybe more so than ever before. Kids are different, parents are different, and coaches are different. And the game is under threat, as I mentioned before. And the only people who can change it are the coaches.

I have always said, of all the coaches today, it is the high school coaches who are the most important. At the high school level, coaches are saving kids' lives; I know that to be true. Some of the kids who enter into football at the high school level don't have a father, and their football coach is the only father they have.

You want to talk about money and what coaches make? Well, that ain't true when it comes to the high school coaches. You want to talk about underpaid people, look at the high school coaches and then look at the responsibilities they have to shape young people's lives. It's terrible what they have a responsibility for and what they make.

My first year at Minnesota, I made $1.2 million to coach football, and my daughter was making $35,000 to $40,000 a year to teach special education kids at the time. Now figure that out. It's not right, but that's what's going on today, and it's not going to change.

I'll say it again: the most important coaches in all sports in our country today are the high school coaches, and they are the most underpaid. It was like that at Webb City when I coached there. For some of those kids, the only thing they had to look forward to in their lives was football. And if that's all a kid has, don't you think how they are coached (and by whom) is important?

Don't get me wrong; what we do at the college level is important too. I mean, coaches change a lot of kids' lives at the college level, but the influence that high school coaches have is greater. From the ages of about 14 to 18, kids are so impressionable, and the influence of teachers and coaches is critical.

I think we have to do a better job in this country of taking care of the people in jobs that have such a great impact on kids. We have to take a much closer look at how we take care of our kids. The school programs need to stress physical conditioning more, and taking care of our bodies as well as our minds. The mind does not work as well if the body doesn't work. They go hand in hand, and I think we have lost track of that connection.

All these things to me are a part of coaching and teaching. Coaching and teaching are the same damn thing. Take Coach Nick Saban at Alabama. There is no doubt Alabama gets the best players and they win a lot of games, but to do that those kids have to be taught. And Coach Saban is a great teacher.

We have to teach kids at all levels. Teaching goes along with coaching, and the commitment by coaches has to be to have the kids be first, not chasing after the almighty dollar. I wish it would all go back to the way it was back in the day. There was never a doubt back then that the kids came first. It was what it was all about. I'm smart enough to realize it will never get back to that again, but we have to understand where we have come from and where we are today. And with that in mind, we have to continue to have the basics of teaching and coaching always be the most important.

Giving all you have every single moment you have a kid under your influence, and pointing that young person in the right direction, is far greater than winning football games. Coaching is so much more than what the dollar will bring. Yes, I love this game. Hell, $40,000 a year? Let's go coach some ball!

eleven

Business and Football

RUNNING A FOOTBALL PROGRAM IS no different than running a business. Certainly coaching at Minnesota in the Big Ten conference might be on a bigger stage than at a smaller school, but the basics and principles of success are the same. And that holds true in business as well. It doesn't matter if it is a Fortune 500 company or a corner hardware store in a small town—there has to be a vision and a mission.

In football we can say things like we want to graduate players and we want to win the conference championship. That's our vision. Well, in a business you have to do the same thing. You have to be able to go in and sit down with your employees and tell them, "This is what we want to have happen. This is our mission."

From that statement you have to go into, "Now, how are you going to get there? What are your core principles of how you are going to get there?" I mean you can have a vision or mission, but you have to have your core principles to work with or it will be meaningless.

For football, number one is accountability. You have to be accountable to yourself and to the program. And if you are in business, you better be accountable, or you will be out of business real fast. It may be in the sales area or the bottom line of how much you are making this month. This helps you get to the mission.

The other core principles that we go by are knowledge and intelligence. Some football people who have not had success do not realize just exactly how smart you have to be and the knowledge you have to have to play the game. If you don't have knowledge of the game, you are not going to win any championships. You have got to have kids who understand what you are doing, and that they can't make mistakes. And that is the accountability part that goes with it. Same for business.

In a business, you are going to have your ups and downs, and things are not always going to go your way, so you have to be mentally tough and even physically tough. If your physical toughness is lacking, it will affect your mental toughness. You have to have core principles that are in place to match up with your mission statement in order to be successful.

From there it goes into team values in that you have to care about your employees. You have to have people who are good teammates who care more about their teammates than they care about themselves. And you have to have strong leadership to be effective.

In a corporation or in football, it cannot be "I-ville"; it has to be "We-ville." Pulling together brings out the rewards. If everyone understands their roles and they work together, then they can accomplish the mission. However, if there are a lot of selfish people who don't understand their roles and don't understand that the more they do, the better the company does—and therefore the more they get rewarded—then you have trouble. And sometimes people like that bring down their company or team.

Leadership qualities are critical. You have the owner of the company, or in some cases you might have co-owners. Or you might have the chief executive officer who runs the company. In football the CEO of the company is the head coach. And the head coach's job is to be accountable to the college president and the athletic director, and to work together with these people to accomplish the mission. Therefore, leadership at the top is essential; without it, failure is on the horizon.

The CEO, or coach, has to then surround himself with the best of the best. This was certainly true with me and the football programs I have taken over. For the most part, these programs were broken-down companies, so to speak. When you have broken-down companies, you have to have people who are going to be loyal, who stay with you and know what the hell they are doing.

And I get asked from time to time, "How do you do that? How do you keep those people and have them be loyal to you?" Well, you have to treat them well and see that they are paid equal to what they are worth. And you have to always think of them before you think of yourself. You think of their families and you make them feel a part of what you are doing by allowing, and giving credit to, their input into the company or program.

The CEO or the head coach also has to be a teacher and teach about the core principles and the mission. Employees have to understand accountability and what they are expected to do. And you have to have different people with different skills. In football, you might have someone who has great skills as a line coach while someone else may be good at recruiting. You have to have good skills from a lot of people in many areas, and this provides balance for you with your team or company.

You may have a great salesperson and have someone else who is a better administrator who will help that salesperson become successful. In football we have an offensive coordinator and we have a defensive coordinator, and they work with their position coaches on each side of the ball to perform their everyday duties to help their football team become successful. And they are provided guidance by the head coach, or on the business side, by the CEO of the company. It is the responsibility of the person in charge to find people to fill these critical roles.

It all trickles down from the top, and each tier has to understand the mission, the core principles, and be able to communicate it successfully. In a company, your assistant coaches are your managers. Those assistant coaches train the players, or in the business sense, the managers train the employees. And the bottom line to this is that the assistant coaches/managers have to get their respective teams to feel good about what they are doing. They have to pass the right knowledge on to them in order to get them to perform on game day. And they have to believe in what their expectations are.

In football or business, people with different responsibilities all have to work together, and communication is the key ingredient for getting that to happen. This is critical.

In today's world, communication comes mostly from cell phones, email, texting, and that kind of thing, but I am old-school with all that in many respects. I believe strongly in communication, but I believe the best results come from face-to-face communication. I understand, of course, that cannot always be done, and for saving time, it may not always be the best way, but when you are talking to someone directly, your chances for success are greater in so many ways.

In football, a lot of mistakes that light up the scoreboard come from a lack of communication. I think kids today are on the cell phones so damn much that if they had them out on the field, as I mentioned earlier, they would probably communicate better. But that's not how you do everyday life if you want good, solid communication.

At the end of a day, a business—or a football team—has to be successful by reaching its mission statement. And if you are not reaching that mission statement, then you have to make adjustments. But those adjustments can't take you away from the core principles.

I have had to make adjustments as a head football coach because the game is always evolving, or sometimes people aren't doing their jobs within the framework of our core principles and mission. People have to keep up. I have done a lot of things to be sure I am in flow with changes that may be made to the game in order to stay on top. It goes with accountability. We want to win football games and graduate players, and a company wants to make money. It's all the same thing.

And to do all this, as I said, you have to be mentally tough, because in football you aren't always going to win. Game day is not different from business. When things are not going your way, you've got to find a way to correct it, and that often hits right at accountability. And how do you hold people accountable? You have to talk with them every day. You have to be around them and communicate with them: "This is what we want to get accomplished today. This is where we want to be at the end of the day." Talk to them. Respect them. Tell them what you want. "This is what we have to be better at. This is what we need to do." Doing this and being around your employees gets you to where you want to be and will make your business tremendous.

And another thing: at the end of the day, in order to be successful, you cannot expect more than your people can handle. I always say that you have to keep things simple, stupid. Don't try to do things that you think should be done if your people are not capable of handling them. Keep it simple and everything will work better. Do the little things, do the fundamentals; keeping it simple in football or business will lead to success.

I keep saying it starts at the top. The example you set is critical. The person at the top is the most important person and must set the best example. The CEO or the head football coach has to work harder than anyone else. It's just that simple. I always did that wherever I was because it's important. I had to show my people that I could outwork everybody, and I wanted to set the tone for others to try to keep up. You have got to be able to make your staff and players understand that hard work brings success.

You cannot tell your staff or players the importance of doing something and then not do it yourself. As the head person, you made the principles, so you must follow them. You have to set the example and be the leader that everyone else follows and looks up to. It's the only way to get people to believe in what you are trying to accomplish. That's what leadership is. The leader sets the pace and the example. I have been successful because I have people who have followed the lead.

If I've got some lazy ass who doesn't want to do his job and I find I can't work with the person, then I've got to let him go. I also think at times it is good to bring in some new blood. Sometimes change and new ideas work toward success.

Good people who work hard will always make mistakes. I make mistakes all the time, and the key is to learn from those mistakes. I always want to work with people and help them learn from their mistakes. I firmly believe that you can't learn anything if you don't make mistakes. Hell, if you aren't making mistakes, then you aren't doing anything.

Now, if you have people who keep making the same mistakes and they can't change their ways, then they have to go. In my football company, I try to give everyone a chance, and as I said, mistakes are a great tool to learn from. People who give their best and understand their mistakes and are willing to learn from them are going to get better and become a greater asset for your company.

As a leader, I sometimes get too involved with my employees, mostly because I am so hands-on. But I have learned a lot over the years, and I want to teach and do it the right way. I see it a lot in football today with these young coaches who have had very little experience and they get these head coaching jobs. And the fact is they don't have the experience or the knowledge to be successful. They don't know everything. When I became a head coach, I had a lot of experience to run the company, and then I surrounded myself with good people.

I had been an offensive coordinator and a defensive coordinator, so I knew what was supposed to go on at each side of the ball. It's the same with business. You have to know what is taking place in all parts of your company. You can't lead and have good followers without knowing that. Still, at the same time, you have to trust and let those good people do their jobs and take ownership of their responsibilities. And if they don't do their jobs, then you have to find people who will.

I mention surrounding yourself with good people. And I am often asked, "How do you find those good people?" I'm a little different from others in the way I hire people, and I don't think that's all bad. What I mean is that I may not personally know the person I hire, but I'm going to know who they worked with in their past.

The important thing is building a good network so if you don't know the person you may hire, you know someone who knows that potential hire. If I have confidence in the person who knows the potential hire, that may be enough for me. I keep my network out there and have people I trust who can tell me what I need to know to make that hiring decision.

You will always have people who are good at interviewing and some who are not. How they perform in the job interview does not always tell you who is going to do the best job for you. That's why you have to do your research and rely on others to give you the information you need to make that critical decision. I can think of a couple people I hired who did not interview very well but are damn good workers with great knowledge and commitment. They had great motivation and were willing to learn. And you can't always determine that with an interview.

If you are running a company that is failing or you are coming into a company that has been failing, the first thing you do is look at your people. In football, when I came into a program, the first thing I looked at was people (the players) and how they were doing with their academics. I wanted to know who was on track to graduate, who had the knowledge, and I went from there. Without my players moving in the right direction, we were not going to win. It's the same thing with a company; you have to look at your people.

I have to have the right people. I talk with them, and if they are the right fit for the company and for what I want to accomplish, I keep them, and if they're not, they've got to go. As I said, sometimes you have to bring in new people. However, to make it work I often had to bring people with me from where I had previously been, because I knew they understood what it was I wanted to accomplish.

This was almost always true. I brought people with me who had proven over the years that they were loyal to me and completely understood what the goals were. I was fortunate to have several coaches who were with me more than 15 years, some more than 20.

It doesn't matter if it's football or business, the key ingredient is the people. Their knowledge, their ability to work together, and their commitment are the keys. Sometimes you have to change the whole culture of an organization to become successful.

Running a business or a football team is not easy. It always starts with the vision and the mission and then having the people who can make it happen by believing in the ultimate goals. It is a constant evaluation process, and if you have the right people with you at all levels in the organization, you have a chance. I evaluate every single day—including myself—and if the evaluations are not good, then I have to fix it. The goal is to win every day!

| twelve |

Loves of My Life

FOOTBALL HAS BEEN A PART of my life for a long time, and it has often taken me away from the most important thing in my life: family. I tried golf some in the past but soon realized that activities like that also took me away from what I love the most.

I have been asked what I like to do in my spare time—I mean time away from football—and although it took me a while to get it figured out, I found what I like to do most is spend time with Rebecca and my girls. There was a time when my life was football, football, and more football. And then when I had a chance to get away from it some, I found a way to get even more football.

But now when I think about the true loves of my life, the first thing that comes to my mind is my family. I know I wouldn't have my family without God in my life, so the two make a great fit for me. There is nothing more important to me than family. I actually can't call my family my hobby; they are my whole life.

I mentioned God in my life, and I know without the good Lord, I wouldn't have my family. So Him, my family, and football—that pretty much sums up my life.

I'll start here with Rebecca. First of all, I don't know who would ever marry me, so she was definitely sent to me from God. And there is no doubt about that. *I* wouldn't marry me. When you talk about getting to heaven, I guarantee that my Rebecca will have a one-way ticket in, no questions asked. I'm not sure of a lot of things in my life, but that is one thing I know to be true.

We met at an early age. I was 21 and she was 19. I had gone for a visit to her hometown of Liberal, Kansas, with her brother, Doug, who was my roommate in college. I told her I was going to marry her at her supper table. Her boyfriend was sitting there at the table with us, so I guess I pretty much must have loved her right from the beginning. I had never met her before, so it must have been one of those gut feelings that I have used for success most of my life.

We got married, and over the years we have been through a lot. We have grown together as the years have gone by, and she is my best friend. In my life, when the chips have been down and things aren't going right or for the best, she's been there.

With all the physical problems I have had with cancer and epilepsy, and all the cycles of medications, it has been Rebecca who has gotten me through everything. She has been with me all the way and been the guiding force keeping me on the right track.

Few people know about Rebecca's passion and commitment to help others. For example, what she did for her brother Don, who was in Minnesota with the rest of her family for the Michigan game a few years back. Don basically died at the stadium that day and was rushed to the hospital with a severe allergic reaction. A month went by and Don never came around, but Rebecca never gave up on him. It's who she is—always there for those who need her. Don was finally taken off life support, with Rebecca right there with him at his hospital bedside. She had been with him every day, just as she has been with our girls and me through some really tough times.

In the beginning, when we first got together, I'm not so sure I was a good fit for Rebecca's family. They likely were thinking, *This isn't the best thing for our daughter.* I don't blame them. She was only 19 and left home to marry a damn football coach. Then she was alone all the time while I worked these insane hours, and then we kept moving from place to place. I understand their side, looking back. But over the years, things got better and we were doing well, had some great jobs, had our wonderful girls, and I guess they must have thought, *Well, she's stuck with him now. We better make the best of it.* I'm just kidding, of course, because as time went by, things turned out well, and now I feel fortunate and blessed to be a part of her family. Rebecca's dad died many years ago, and her mom, Mary Lois Smith, and I have a great relationship.

As I look back over the years, it is Rebecca who continues to hold down the place as the rock in our family. She was the supreme caregiver for me when I went through my bout with cancer and continues now with my epilepsy. I honestly don't know how I would have gotten through everything without her.

And with all my players, she is so special. Many of my guys over the years have thought of her as their second mom, and she's earned the nickname Momma Kill.

I feel bad for her and my girls for all they have gone through. I hope when it is time for one of us to go, I go first, because I wouldn't know what the hell to do without her. She does it all. She keeps the checkbook, runs the house, and keeps it all together. She has done it all while I coached football. That's about all I did. That's the straight-up truth. I mean, I may not have anything. She may have spent it all. Hell, I wouldn't know.

It is one of those things where I never cared much about money. I cared about others most of the time. I really did. If you look at it closely, I probably spent more time with, and helping, other young people than I did my own kids. Every coach does that with all the time they are away from their families; it's just the way it is.

I will guarantee you Rebecca has seen things that no woman should ever see with all my seizures and health issues. And through it all, she has done a great job raising our kids. And our kids are the best. I know everyone says that about their kids, but we do have great kids.

I think over the years as adversity hit us, we became tighter and stronger as a couple, and also as a family. I think we all became closer and learned from our experiences together. I think, like I mentioned before, early on in our marriage, Rebecca wasn't sure she wanted to be part of this crazy football world, and she left for a short time. I know there were many things I should have done better—and things I should still do better—but I worked on them with her, and here we are today. We got it figured out, and I honestly don't know what I would have done over the years without her being at my side.

Rebecca, through everything, has been the one. There weren't a lot of people volunteering to be with me during the tough times in my life, that's for sure. It has always been Rebecca. She is a great listener. She is not the type to always share a lot of information; she just listens. She is a great person.

During the critical times, she was there, giving the right advice. She never told me what to do. She never said, "You need to do this. You need to quit football. You should do it this way." She always put things in the right perspective: "Do the right thing for our family."

Rebecca protected me in the past and does it today. She guides me in the right direction. She handles everything and controls all the medical parts of my life as the best caregiver ever. I wouldn't be here today without Rebecca. She is the rock that holds it all together for me and our family. I don't know where I would be today without Rebecca; she is truly the love of my life.

I mentioned my wonderful daughters, Krystal and Tasha. They are great kids. Krystal is the oldest, our first. She was born when I was coaching at Pittsburg State. There were some complications during her birth, and I was actually the first one to get to hold

Krystal because of Rebecca's situation. And Krystal had some difficulties early on, but we got through it all, and I sure latched on to her. She was our first child and I was her dad, and that's a special thing.

Krystal is really something. She loves football. I think if she could, she probably would want to be a football coach. She has been on the sideline with me for the better part of 20 years. She loved it and I loved it. She held the communication cords for me, and kept them from getting tangled up, from the time she was seven years old. And I'll tell you, with me running all over and up and down the sideline, that was no easy task.

I remember during a game at Saginaw Valley State, she got wiped out. I mean she got hit from the side and got rolled up. I told her, "Aw, just toughen up and you'll be all right." So when we went in at halftime, she went and found her mother and teared up some, but when we came back out, there she was with me on the sideline. She is a tough girl. And I almost forgot to mention that when she got clobbered and hit the ground, she never let go of those cords!

When Krystal was playing sports, she had some major surgery for a torn ACL playing softball and played her junior year when she wasn't really supposed to. Like I said, she is tough. Another time, I remember I got in some trouble with Rebecca because Krystal was playing soccer and broke her toe. Rebecca called me from the game and told me, "Well, she broke her toe, and here, talk to the doctor." The doctor was at the game because he had a daughter playing too. The team was already short on players, and Krystal was hurt. The doctor said, "Coach, what do you think? She has this broken toe, and there's not a whole lot we can do." And I said, "Hell, play her. She's tough enough to play. Play her."

Well, Rebecca didn't talk to me for a while after that one. I guess she didn't agree with me on my decision for her to play. "Play her" would not have been the call Rebecca would have made.

Krystal is a good athlete and now works in the city with special education kids. That's her love in life, helping kids who really need her help. She is the type who, whenever there is someone in need of help, she will be there for them. She is that kind of person. She is the kindest person you will ever meet. She is a good girl.

As I look ahead with her, she will probably find ways in her life to take care of this person and that person. If there is a stray dog around, she'll take it in; that's just her nature. She would try to save the world if that was possible. I mean, she would.

Tasha is our baby girl. She was born in Joplin, Missouri, when I was coaching, and it was the same year we won the national championship. The funny thing about Krystal and Tasha is that growing up Krystal was the country girl and Tasha was the little petite thing, no country in her. And now it has switched. Tasha is out in the country living, and Krystal is in the city. It really doesn't make a whole lot of sense, but that's how kids change.

Krystal has a lot of her mother's traits, while Tasha and I are a lot alike. Tasha is like a rattlesnake. When she got married, I knew who was running that marriage. She has a lot of fire in her. And another thing about her: she will protect her daddy. If someone should say something bad about me, she'll go after them. No doubt about that. She is highly intelligent and does a great job as a speech pathologist.

I recall at her wedding she did something really special for me. I had to get all that gear and stuff on that you wear for a wedding. I hate dressing up with that stuff, and they made me get dressed early too. Then they made me get to the church early. When we got there way ahead of time, I said, "Why did I have to put all this stuff on so early, and why are we at the church so early?" They walked me through the doors and I saw Tasha at the front of the church, standing right where she was going to get married.

They told me to walk up to Tasha. When I got there, she held my hand and pulled out this piece of paper and read to me what she thought of her dad and all that we had been through together.

I guess I'm not so tough after all, because halfway through that letter I lost it. I mean, I tried to talk to her and I couldn't. I left the church and got myself together and was all right to walk her down the aisle. But it was something. I'll never forget what that letter meant to me at the time and forever after. And we had the father-daughter dance and that was special. It was a great day.

I'm a pretty protective dad. I was definitely the type who made dating one of my daughters tough and a real experience. Coming to that front door at the Kills' to take one of my girls out was not easy. "Hey, you touch my daughter or do anything to hurt her and I'll kick your ass." But other than that, I was pretty good. But there was not a lot of dating in high school at the Kill house. I guess college was better for them, because they were away from me.

I have to say that despite me and all my protectiveness, Tasha did meet a great young man by the name of Jason Hynes. He is a real special person, and as a dad I could not be more pleased with who Tasha picked for her husband. Jason is a hard worker and reminds me in so many ways of my brother, Frank. I have to laugh as I think back on all the times he was going to ask me for my daughter's hand in marriage. Something would always seem to come up. He would be ready, and then we would lose a football game or whatever. He finally picked the time to ask me when I was elected to the Hall of Fame. He hit on a good time, and I love to tease him about it. He is, without question, the best son-in-law I could ever ask for. I'm very proud of him.

Krystal and Tasha, I am so thankful for each of them. I don't know how I would get along without my girls. Both are my special angels. I have won a lot of football games in my life, but the best wins Rebecca and I have ever enjoyed are our two girls. My memories of and with them are as important to me as anything I have ever enjoyed. I cannot begin to say how absolutely fortunate I am to have Rebecca, Krystal, and Tasha in my life.

I have always been honest about my life. I have always told others the importance of family and to make sure they take care of them and put them first, because I didn't always do that. When the chips are down and the day comes to an end, no one else cares but your family and close friends. They are the ones that will be there for you during the best of times and the worst of times. And in a family, the thing you will cherish most is those kids. They will grow up fast, and someday you will look around and say, "Where the hell did all that time go?"

When I speak to groups, family is at the forefront. I know there were so many times I missed things in life because of what I do and who I am. I feel bad about that at times, but I try to keep in mind it's who I am. Still, I know how important family is.

Sometimes I think I messed up by cheating my kids with my time. But then at the same time I try to think they have gotten a lot out of life that other kids will never get because of my coaching.

Above anything else—I mean winning football games and championships and all that—first comes family and a deep-rooted caring for people. Without that ingrained in my heart and soul, I haven't got much else.

| thirteen |
Faith, Family, and Football

THROUGHOUT MY LIFE I HAVE been a person of faith. I was raised by faithful parents and married into Rebecca's family of devout churchgoers, very faithful people. Rebecca and I have continued our journey in the same direction.

However, I want to make sure that people understand that through that journey, keeping the right order of faith, family, and football has at times become clouded. Maintaining my faith first, followed closely by family, often was leapfrogged by football.

I feel it is sometimes easy for people, myself included, to say they are maintaining a proper order, but the reality is, it is very difficult to do what you say or believe in this regard. It seems that other influences often find a way to interfere, especially if you have great passion for your line of work, as I had in 32 years of coaching football.

Over the years in my profession, I have had the opportunity to work with people like Tubby Smith, when he was basketball coach at Minnesota, and I learned from his faith and commitment. Tubby has it figured out and lives his life with faith, family, and work in the right order. And that's why he is such a special person and I respect him so much.

Roger Lipe, our chaplain when I was at Southern Illinois, is another person who has that clear understanding of what's important in life. He has it figured out too.

Keeping people like Tubby and Roger in mind, I try my best to be like them, and I'm still working on it every single day. They are on the right track and I'm trying to catch up, and I'm making progress every day. I really am.

I will say this: It has been my faith and Rebecca's faith that have gotten us through the adversity that we have faced, and we have faced many difficult times. Our marriage has been blessed by the faith we have had. During early marriage difficulties, we relied on a priest and friends to give us the right guidance. When I faced great physical difficulties the day before I resigned at the University of Minnesota, I talked with a priest.

When the cancer hit me, it was a gigantic wake-up call, and let me tell you, you get your life straightened out pretty fast with that diagnosis. It was the same with the epilepsy, but it shouldn't work that way. You shouldn't have to experience a major event in your life to get your priorities back in order. There should not be such a thing in your life as a wake-up call. I can tell you from my experiences, life is so much better when your faith stands above everything else.

When things were going the very best for me at Minnesota and I was on a roll physically, mentally, and professionally, I was eating right, exercising right, and going to church every day. I had my priorities in the right lineup. My daily church attendance was special for me, and it brought me back to what I always knew: faith, family, and then football. But then I let it slip and it took a while to get my order back.

My faith has enlightened me to some extent as to the reason I am here. I hope to learn more. I mean I had Stage 4 cancer, epilepsy, and have at times been in pretty rough shape. But I'm here, and there is a reason for me still being around. I believe that with all my heart, and I know God will provide me the guidance and resolve to find what it is. I know for sure it is to help people, to give back. But how and when and where? I believe I will receive the answers.

I believe that cancer came into my life so that Rebecca and I would start the Coach Kill Cancer Fund. I believe epilepsy came into my life so Rebecca and I would start the Chasing Dreams Coach Kill Epilepsy Fund. We are supposed to give back, and our faith has provided the guidance in that regard.

Faith has been such a big part of my life, but as an honest person, I have to say I have not always had the priorities I talk about in the correct order. I have let them slip away and then struggled to get them back. And in the process, it is easy to realize that without faith and family, nothing else works. The best years of my life have come with faith, family, and football, in that order.

Count Your Blessings
Count your blessings instead of your crosses;
Count your gains instead of your losses.
Count your yeses instead of your nos;
Count your friends instead of your foes.
Count your smiles instead of your tears;
Count your courage instead of your fears.
Count your full years instead of your lean;
Count your kind deeds instead of your mean.
Count your health instead of your wealth;
Count on God instead of yourself.
                    —Author Unknown

fourteen

Principles for Life

1. Honesty and 2. Integrity

Honesty and integrity are critical to me. Today, I think they are a lost art. I want these words connected to the name Jerry Kill because they are that important. Doing what you say you are going to do and having people believe in you is what life is all about. These are the key ingredients to being successful.

3. Do the Right Thing

You know when you are doing right. I mean, do what you are supposed to do. I tell my players and coaches in such a simple and clear way…just do what is right. Do the right thing. That's all you have to do, and the fact is, we all know what is right and what is wrong.

4. What Have You Done to Better Yourself Today?

Why would you want to stay the same? We cannot worry about yesterday, because it's over and we have to deal with today. Tomorrow isn't here yet, so don't worry about that. But today we are present, so why wouldn't you want to get better?

5. Loyalty

Loyalty begins when someone cares more about someone else than they care about themselves. To me, you have to earn loyalty, and I am loyal to the people who have worked their asses off for me. I want people around me who are going to take care of me, and in turn I will take care of them. If people are loyal to me, let me tell you something: I will always have their back.

6. Do What You Say You Are Going to Do

If you say you are going to do something, do it! Your word is your bond. Don't write the check you can't cash. It is better not to say anything than to fail to follow through on what you say. Accountability is who you are. If someone counts on you to do something, you step up to the plate and do what has to be done. It's an unwritten promise. When people say they are going to do something and they don't do it, they have lost my respect.

7. Build Relationships

It's all about people. I don't care if you're white, black, green, or purple. I don't care about your age, or if you have an earring in your nose. It doesn't matter to me what your job is. It's all about people and the connections you make with them. Everyone can teach everyone else. You can't prejudge people, and you have to find the right relationships with the right kind of people.

8. Be Genuine

Just remember where you came from. Don't try to be something you're not. Don't be a fake. Be yourself. God put you on this planet to be who you are. You have been given tools to be successful, so use those tools.

9. What Is Winning?

Winning football games is important, and no one likes winning more than I do. Losing absolutely kills me. But there is a lot more to winning than being victorious in football games. It's what happens down the road to those players or people you come in contact with. Winning football games won't be on your tombstone, but how many kids or others you helped down the road is what your life will be measured by.

10. Preparation

Be prepared for everything you do. It is important to know what it is you are going into or taking on. Your reputation, success, and credibility have a lot to do with how prepared you are for the largest and smallest of tasks. We may have been on the losing end of some of our football games, but it was never because we were not prepared. Preparation is time-consuming and often difficult, but in the end, it is well worth it.

11. Consistency

Be consistent. Let people know they can count on you and depend on you. It is important in life to value the importance of doing things the same way and the correct way. Consistency builds credibility and is necessary to succeed in your work and your life. As an example, be on time. Never be late. Be consistent!

12. Communication

People don't talk to each other anymore. Talk to people. Communicate with them. Let them know how you think and how you feel. I cannot say enough about the importance of communication and the valuable effect it has on everyone around you. Teamwork starts with communication, both in the workplace and at home with your family.

13. Adversity

How do you react when things aren't going the right way? How do you react when your back is against the wall? How do you respond when things aren't going well? What do you do? This is how success is truly measured. Be the kind of person who handles the toughest times with great character and resolve. This is when toughness comes into play. Be your best at the worst of times. When the going is tough, the tough get going!

14. Intelligence vs. Knowledge

I want smart people working for me—intelligent people, people who are willing to learn. People do not have to know everything to be intelligent. They have to be willing to learn, like a sponge ready to soak everything in. In coaching, I could teach those who were smart, motivated, and willing to learn. Your success and their success depends on it.

15. Faith and Family First

The most important thing in your life will always be your faith and your family, and they have to always be first, before anything else. Once you let them slip in your priorities, it can be hard to make up the lost time. Keep them in the right place.

16. Put Others First

Put other people and their best interests before your own. When you do, other things—such as loyalty—fall into place.

17. Be Thankful

Take the time to look around and be thankful for what you have, because it can go away real fast.

18. A Reason for Everything

I think there is a reason for everything. God has a plan for all of us. I know what has happened to me in my life with football, cancer, and epilepsy has happened for a reason, and I'm prepared to find out what that reason is.

19. Trust Your Faith

I live on Faith Drive in southern Illinois, and it fits well with my faith and my beliefs. God has a plan for me and my family, and I have faith in that plan so I can act on it appropriately.

20. Toughness

Toughness doesn't have to be just in football or sports. I mean mental and physical toughness. I would tell my players, "We are going to be tougher than anyone else, mentally and physically." When the chips are down in business, football, or life, toughness has to prevail, and it's what makes people successful.

fifteen

Famous Killisms

I HAVE ALWAYS BEEN TOLD that my use of words and phrases is quite unique. In fact, it has been mentioned to me that I am responsible for rewriting the English language. As a result of that, some of my closest colleagues compiled a list of my most commonly used "Killisms":

- I'm too busy burnin' out fires!
- It's rainin' like a striped-ass ape out there
- We need to break up the mentality [monotony]
- Wicked Witch of the East
- His strength is his Achilles' tendency
- Are there any airplane wars going on out there so we can get some cheaper flights?
- He's got more family shit goin' on than the man on the moon
- You're going to be a turd in a punchbowl!
- You need to insert [assert] yourself
- It just kinda murderizes us 'cause we don't have a kicker
- Those kids should be ready to go injury-wise, as far as being on the Richter scale

- Krystal was crushed when we went headless this year; she couldn't carry a wire
- We're going to give him a scholarship, but there may be some stimulations [stipulations] to it
- We're caught between a hard and a rock spot
- Uglier than a mud fence
- I'm going to hell in a handcart!
- I think he was trying to pull the wool under my eyes
- I don't want to bring you here and pull the bullshit over your eyes
- Call and put out an ABP [APB] on that kid
- We're pissin' down a rope
- That gym floor is not very good…it will be a slick fest out there
- Swallow the frog, make a decision
- Give that guy an apple and a road map; he can get out of town
- You look like a mouse turd—sharp on both ends
- If they put your brains in a jaybird's ass, it would fly backward
- You're as soft as Dairy Queen ice cream
- You wouldn't hit a dead snake
- You are a cake eater
- It's raining like a cow pissing on a flat rock
- You only live once, so you better enjoy it
- They are stacked up like club sandwiches
- That son of a buck is faster than my car
- Get that piano off his back
- You don't get fired for spending money; you get fired for losing football games
- Finish! Finish! Finish!
- You can fall in a basket of shit and come out looking like a rose
- Ball security, job security

- He couldn't throw the damn thing in the ocean
- You can't make chicken salad out of chicken shit
- Is there any light at the end of the tunnel?
- She would make a bulldog break his chain
- All the kids in the village are proud of you
- Do the right thang
- No matter what—win, lose, or draw—I love ya!
- Care about the person next to you more than yourself
- Good players make good coaches
- Coaches don't win games; players do
- You have to look good to feel good to play good
- He plays like a blind dog in a meat house
- You are the best thing since a slice of bread
- Don't *tell* me what you can do; show me!
- I will kick your ass until you bark like a fox
- He doesn't have a pot to piss in
- This storm is going to be a toad strangler
- You're as stiff as a broomstick
- You have got to be shitting me
- Play like your hair is on fire
- They aren't going to put wins and losses on your tombstone
- You'll be judged by how you have treated others

[Coauthor's note: This ends the Killisms...for now. Fortunately there is a deadline for the manuscript of Coach Kill's book or his list would never end. He comes up with two or three new Killisms every day!]

| sixteen |
Final Thoughts

IN WRITING THIS BOOK, I wanted to express my appreciation and everlasting gratitude to all those people who have come into my life along the way, including but not limited to all my colleagues and players in football, my many friends and associates, my multiple friends involved in my cancer and epilepsy funds, the great football fans at all the stops I have made, and my wonderful family.

My hope in my book was to express my deepest passions for the great game of football and to illustrate that through hard work and commitment, anything is possible. I wanted to point out the importance of always remembering where we came from and that reaching out to assist others is the real pinnacle and measurement of success.

Having had the opportunity to take on a number of missions and responsibilities over the past three decades, I have been truly blessed with being associated with great people, incredible loyalty, and a profound faith that has helped me to understand the real important things in life.

I hope that joining me in my journey has been interesting and meaningful for you, and I want to thank you. It's been a wonderful ride, and it's only the beginning.

Afterword *by the Kill Family*

JERRY AND I HAD A very interesting first meeting. When we tell people the story, I know they think it can't be true…but it absolutely is! Jerry was my brother Doug's roommate in college. I was in high school at the time, and my brother came to our home in Liberal, Kansas, one evening with Jerry and a few other friends to watch some football games.

That night my mom fixed dinner for everyone and we were all sitting at the table. My brother was there, my boyfriend was there, and Jerry was there. Well, before Doug, Jerry, and the others left to watch football, Jerry told my brother in front of everybody that he was going to marry me. There was total silence in the room.

After I graduated from high school I went to the same college Jerry and two of my brothers were attending, and they came over to help me move in. I was still dating my boyfriend from home, but after a while we broke up.

Jerry and I had become great friends, and after I broke up with my boyfriend, Jerry and I began dating and eventually married. Much later I found out from Jerry's mom that he had come home that weekend when he had first met me and told her he found the person he was going to marry. And that's the truth.

Our first few years together were very rough because of all the time Jerry spent coaching football and away from home. Jerry was gone all the time. He would leave for work at 6:00 in the morning and not get home some nights until midnight. At first I remember many times wondering, *What in the world did I get myself into?* I was young, and this was all new to me. I had no idea what it was like to be a football coach's wife.

We worked it out. We went to some counseling, and after we had our girls it was so much easier on me. I had responsibility over our children, and I loved being around them and taking care of them.

Moving at times can be difficult, especially with children, but we have met so many wonderful people in every place we have been. Probably one of the toughest moves we made was from Southern Illinois to Northern Illinois, because Tasha was a senior in high school and she stayed back with friends to complete her senior year. It was tough on all of us, but it worked out. I would drive every week back to Carterville to be with Tasha during the week and then back to DeKalb to be with Jerry on the weekends.

I think all the changes were good for us. I believe they helped our girls adjust to new places and things. It gave them the opportunity to meet a lot of people and do things they may never have had a chance to do if we had stayed in one place.

As tough as everything was in the beginning for Jerry and me, I wouldn't change anything for the world. It has been such a great experience. We have been fortunate to always live in really nice places, around great people. I loved living in the Twin Cities because it was so new to me. I had never lived in a big city before, so it was a wonderful experience.

I especially loved living in Southern Illinois, mostly because we lived in that area the longest. Our girls pretty much grew up there, and we really have called it our home over the years. We have a lake place there and made so many friends all over the area.

My mom lives near Kansas City now, and I have had the opportunity to see her more often recently. She was able to get to some games along with my family and stayed with us for a while, and that was special to me. Family has always been very important to Jerry and me, so we take the time to be with them as much as we can. Mom is 90 years old, so we know the importance of being with her, the same as with Jerry's mom; having them both in our lives is a real blessing.

When I found out Jerry had cancer, it felt like it hit us all at once. I had been around people in my life who had the disease, but never someone so close to me. As Jerry mentioned earlier in this book, we found out about the cancer because of his epilepsy. If he had not had the seizure and been transported to the hospital, we never would have found out about the cancer. Although it was a very difficult time, without question, we were significantly blessed.

The doctors had been working with us for about a week to try to find out about the seizure. We didn't know much about seizures or epilepsy then, so this was all new to us. There were so many questions, such as, "What caused this to happen?" and "Will this happen again?" It was all really confusing and scary. And then came the cancer.

During those times, I thought, *Is my husband and the girls' father going to be with us?* It was very difficult to tell our girls what was going on back then, because they really didn't understand it all.

Jerry's cancer was Stage 4, but it was positioned in his body in a way that it could be taken out, so it all worked out. After Jerry's surgery to remove the cancer, through my faith in God, I started to truly believe this was all supposed to happen for a reason. God does act in mysterious ways sometimes, and for us it was a great blessing. God had a plan. If Jerry had not had that seizure, we may not have found out about the cancer until it was too late. Things fell positively into place for us.

Overall the epilepsy has been much more difficult to deal with. With cancer you can learn about it and get to understand how it will be treated. Epilepsy is much harder to comprehend, and most people don't really understand all that goes with it.

As the years have gone on, I have learned more and more about epilepsy. I know what to do if Jerry has a seizure, and I have a better understanding of what the disease is all about. It was quite a while before I learned that someone can actually die from a seizure. I knew it was serious, but it came as a shock to me when I first learned that a seizure could possibly take my husband from me. After a seizure, I always thought, *Okay, he is going to be okay now, and we can move on*. I had no idea of the grave nature of epilepsy and that a seizure could be so critical to one's life.

While at the University of Minnesota, Jerry was on a much larger platform, and I believe this was in God's plans for us too. Because of that larger stage, Jerry's epilepsy and cancer got nationwide attention, which has allowed us to reach out and help so many people who are suffering with life-changing illnesses.

After Jerry beat his cancer, we were able to help so many others with our Coach Kill Cancer Fund. And with epilepsy, he is fortunate not to have it as bad as some. Therefore it gives him the opportunity to reach out to so many others with our Coach Kill Chasing Dreams Epilepsy Fund. I believe all that has happened to us has given us the opportunity and enabled us to reach so many others who are in need.

Everything we went through leading up to Jerry's retirement put us in a position at this point where we can really figure out what is next for us. I think the issues that led to Jerry retiring from coaching were in God's plan; God has guided us to this point in our lives, and he has something else in mind for us now. And even though it was a very difficult time to get through, the future is so bright. And whatever it holds, we will be ready for it.

So many things that have happened to us over the past few years happened for the right reasons, even if it didn't at first appear that way. Take the Jim Souhan article in the *Minneapolis Star Tribune*, for instance. As hurtful as that article was, I've moved on from it. And the rallying it prompted at the football games, in Los Angeles, New York, and other places served a tremendous purpose to bring about awareness to epilepsy all over the world. That article brought about anger and support for Jerry that created an awareness for epilepsy like nothing we ever could have imagined.

Another aspect of my life I wanted to mention is being a mom and raising my wonderful daughters, Krystal and Tasha. At times it was tough being a mom and being married to a football coach. I think some of the toughest times were when the girls were young, especially during recruiting season, because Jerry was gone so much. When Jerry was away from home recruiting, even with the girls around me, it was difficult, especially at night. During the regular football season he always worked long hours, but he was usually home at night, and that was important to me.

For the most part during that particular time, I felt like I was a single parent raising my girls. At the same time, I have often thought it was also good, because I was there for them all the time. As the girls got older, though, it got easier. I was fortunate to be able to get a job and work part-time, but the part I enjoyed the most was being there for them and being their mom.

I look at Krystal and Tasha, and my first thought is, *Beautiful girls and beautiful people.* They have turned out to be great and caring human beings. I think we have raised them the right way, and I couldn't be more proud of them. Our lives center around the girls, and each and every day we are thankful we have them. They are our life's greatest blessings.

The adversity our family has had to overcome, coupled with the ups and downs of football, has taught our girls many of life's lessons. They have learned that everything is not always perfect and that sometimes struggles help you learn how to handle some of the difficulties in life. It has all worked out. As I have said before many times, I wouldn't change a thing. I love my life.

Another way our family has been blessed is that the various moves we have made have been by our choice. And that is a huge thing. Some coaches we know have lost their jobs, been fired, and then had to find work wherever they could.

Another thing I have been blessed with in this regard is the way Jerry has handled everything. When he did have the time away from football, he was there with us. He never really took any of his free time for himself. He was with the girls and me, and that was huge for us and for him, because that was the most important thing to all of us. He didn't have any hobbies, so to speak. His hobby was us.

My role as a football coach's wife was so much more than cheering at football games. Especially as the girls got older, I had more time to get involved in the community and with the players in various ways. In some respects, especially in the most recent years, I became sort of a players' mom, and that made me feel like I was part of the program.

I was able to reach out and be there for them. I would text with them and be available to help out when I could. So many of these young players were away from home and needed a mother figure around, and I tried to fill that role for them. To have some of those players call me Momma Kill is very special to me. I love them all like they are my own.

I also feel my role as a head coach's wife was to ensure that other coaches' wives and families felt a sense of belonging. With that grew a special bond over the years, and we developed a kind of extended family. So many of us have been together for so long that we truly have become a large family. The coaches' wives and families are all very important to me, and I hope they know I carry a special place in my heart for each and every one of them. They are truly wonderful people who affected my life in so many wonderful ways, and with whom I've formed relationships I will always cherish. I love each and every one of you. Thanks for all the memories!

As I look back on my family's life together and some of the really tough times, there probably is nothing that compares to the day that Jerry retired from football. It was the hardest day in the world to see him get up there and tell his coaches, his players, and everyone else that he couldn't continue to coach the way he wanted to coach. I was okay with his decision, but to watch him tell everyone was heartbreaking for our family.

The decision, even though I believe it was the right one, was terribly difficult. It was really tough on Krystal and Tasha to watch their dad go through something like that. And for Krystal, it ended almost 20 years of being on the sideline next to her dad on football Saturdays. To watch Jerry's emotions and what he went through was something that will stay with me forever. But as I have said, there was a reason for all this, and as a family, we will be stronger because of it. I really believe that.

I'm not sure what the future holds. I'm not really a look-ahead kind of person. I kind of go day-to-day. Jerry is feeling so much better now. We have been able to get some exercise together and have been able to do things we never had the time to do before. Best of all, we have found more time to enjoy our kids; we are spending more time with them now than we have for a long time.

Who knows what is in store for us in the future? There are a lot of possibilities for Jerry and me. I'm very positive about it all. In fact, I'm excited!

—Rebecca Kill

BEING THE DAUGHTERS OF A football coach is indescribable. It has shaped both of us into the people we are today. Football taught us many life lessons, but most important, it taught us love: the love of the game, the love of a coach for his players, the love amongst players as they become brothers, and the relationships we built with all the families who embraced the journey along with us.

When our dad had to retire from coaching, we both had mixed emotions. We love the game of football. It's a lifestyle for us. Football had been our whole life and our parents' whole life. Our dad retiring was not easy. However, we knew it was the best thing for him. As he struggled, we also faced the same struggles.

We have faced many battles throughout our dad's coaching career. His cancer diagnosis and epilepsy were two of the hardest, obviously. Through both, we had to count on each other, hold each other up, and stand up for each other. We would be lying if we said there have not been dark times, where we both asked, "Why him? Why our dad?" However, without our family facing these battles, we would not have the relationship we do today. We have grown closer as a family and have all become better people. We have taken the worst of times and made the best out of them.

Our life of being the football coach's daughters has been quite the adventure, but if you ask either of us, we wouldn't want to be part of any other journey.

There are no words to describe what our dad means to us, nor enough pages in this book. We love him more than he will ever know.

Krystal and Tasha's Favorite Memories

Tasha's favorite memories: I share two very special memories with my dad. When I was little my dad and I were in our garden in Saginaw, Michigan, and I remember looking up to him and saying, "Dad, I will always be your little girl." I believe my dad's heart melted at that very moment. My second-favorite memory of my dad happened recently. It was May 23, 2015, the day he walked me down the aisle. I will cherish these two memories for the rest of my life.

Krystal's favorite memories: I have many memories spanning my dad's football career. However, there are two of them that stand out to me. I was on the sideline with him for many of the 32 years he coached. I will never forget when I got tackled on the sideline. I was holding his headphone cord when I got tackled, and I still had the cord in my hand when I went down and when I got back up! I never let that cord go and I never let my dad down. I also never will forget the last game I was on the sideline with my dad. He told me, "You've been with me all these years, and I want to go out with you."

—Krystal Kill and Tasha Hynes

Jerry Kill By the Numbers

.605 Winning percentage as a collegiate head coach (125–99)

1 National Championship. Won as offensive coordinator at Pittsburg State University in 1991

1 Big Ten Coach of the Year (Hayes-Schembechler Coach of the Year and Dave McClain Coach of the Year) at Minnesota in 2014

2 Mid-American Conference Vern Smith Leadership Award (MVP) winners in three years at NIU

3 National Coach of the Year honors. 2007 Liberty Mutual Coach of the Year, 2004 Eddie Robinson Coach of the Year, 2014 Tom Lemming Coach of the Year

3 Bowl-eligible teams in three seasons at Northern Illinois University. 2008 Independence Bowl; 2009 International Bowl; 2010 Humanitarian Bowl

3 Bowl-eligible team in four seasons at Minnesota. 2012 Meineke Car Care Bowl; 2013 Texas Bowl; 2015 Buffalo Wild Wings Citrus Bowl

4 AFCA Regional Coach of the Year honors. 2003 and 2004 at Southern Illinois, 2013 and 2014 at Minnesota

5 NCAA Football Championship Subdivision Playoff appearances as head coach at Southern Illinois University

6 NFL Draft picks in his tenure at Minnesota

7 First-team All–Big Ten selections in his tenure at Minnesota

10 First-team All-MAC selections in his three-year tenure at Northern Illinois

15 Winning seasons (out of 21) as a collegiate head coach

How to Help Others
Chase Their Dreams

I HAVE SAID MANY TIMES before that my cancer and epilepsy may be two of the best things that ever happened to me. Over the course of years I have met many people who are going through the same sorts of things as me, but do not have the resources I am blessed with. Rebecca and I created these funds as a way to help those people in need. Through them we have been able to help so many families, as well as educate people about epilepsy. One in 26 people suffer from epilepsy, and yet most people know so little about it! We're bound and determined to change that.

To find out more about the Chasing Dreams Coach Kill Epilepsy Fund and the Coach Kill Cancer Fund, or to make a donation, visit the websites or call the phone numbers below.

Chasing Dreams Coach Kill Epilepsy Fund
Epilepsy Foundation of Minnesota
www.efmn.org/chasingdreams
(612) 804-5545

Coach Kill Cancer Fund
Southern Illinois Healthcare
www.coachkillfund.org
(618) 457-5200, ext. 67841

More Praise for Jerry Kill

"Coach Kill brought a winner attitude to Minnesota, not a winning attitude.... He made us all winners, and from there winning became a part of it. Few people can do what he has done."
—George Adzick, director of the M Club at the University of Minnesota

"After Coach Kill retired, I was crushed.... If I had only one word to describe Coach Kill, the word would be 'greatness.' I have never seen him give up on a player. I recall a kid one time who I truly believed had no chance. Coach Kill never gave up on him, and that kid is now strength coach at a major university."
—Brian Anderson, assistant coach, University of Minnesota

"If you are in his circle, you have a friend for life."
—Tim Beck, former player and coach, Pittsburg State University

"He is a tough guy, a fighter, and a great football coach. When I think about him, I think about greatness!"
—Briean Boddy-Calhoun, former player

"He has one of the greatest offensive football minds that I have ever been around."
—Chuck Broyles, former head coach, Pittsburg State University

"I spent a lot of time with Coach Kill when he was our head football coach.... When you are around him you can see the fire in his eyes and all of his passion. He is always a fighter, [someone] who cares deeply about young people. I love the man."
—Jim Carter, former Gophers player

"I had covered Major League Baseball for a number of years before I got the Gophers football beat... My contacts with him were as easy as talking to my next-door neighbor. He is as homegrown and as genuine a person as you will ever meet.... I have been so impressed with Jerry and the impact he has had on his players, the students, the state and perhaps most importantly, the epilepsy community. He has been an inspiration to everyone that he comes in contact with."
—Joe Christensen, *Minneapolis Star Tribune*

"To have been in the positions that he has been in with no ego is very rare. He is without a doubt the greatest leader I have ever known.... Coach Kill shaped me as a man."

—Jon Christenson, former player

"He is as competitive and caring as a person can get. He always made decisions best for others and the team, never for himself. We have been through a lot together over the years, just two guys from Kansas."

—Tracy Claeys, head coach, University of Minnesota

"Coach Kill is truly a genuine human being. There is no better man that I know.... I am one of those who would run through a wall for him and do anything for him."

—Adam Clark, director of football operations, University of Minnesota

"He is a tough football coach and was on me all the time, but he encouraged me continually and was always concerned about my future."

—David Cobb, former player

"There are so [many] positives to say about him. He became a father and big brother figure to me when I walked on from the military at Northern Illinois. He never gives up on anyone, and I saw this over and over with him. He is a fighter and fights for you, never allowing you to give anything but your best."

—Jake Coffman, former player

"After I was diagnosed with cancer [Coach Kill]...came into my life. And although I never was on the football field as a player with him, he never gave up on me.... During my toughest times, he was there for me, counseling me and encouraging me. He assisted me with getting the best medical help possible at the Mayo Clinic, of which I will be forever grateful.... I'm doing well now and will always be thankful that Coach Kill came into my life."

—Connor Cosgrove, former player, University of Minnesota

"I have only known Coach Kill for about three years, but he sure has had an impact on me."

—Mark Dantonio, head coach, Michigan State University

"He used to get down on one knee and talk to the team and seemingly to each player at the same time. That was very special! The day Jerry was hired at Minnesota, I told Joel Maturi that he had made a great hire. I was sure right."

—Gerry DiNardo, former head coach, Purdue, and Big Ten Network analyst

"[My son] Billy had never heard of anyone having seizures besides himself.... He clung to Coach as an example of someone with epilepsy doing amazing things—that he was a football coach unafraid to have a seizure in front of thousands of people.... In October 2014, Billy and I traveled from our home in Atlanta to Minneapolis for the Epilepsy Awareness Game against Ohio State.... We walked through the door and [the players] formed a line to give Billy high fives and small words of encouragement.... Coach Kill came over, hugged Billy and gave him an autographed Minnesota helmet. 'You're my hero,' it said. Billy rubbed Coach's head for good luck. On game day, Billy got exclusive access to everything: the locker room, the field, press box. Running back David Cobb pledged to score two touchdowns for Billy and sealed his promise with a giant hug. David scored three touchdowns that day. On the field, punter Pete Mortell played catch with Billy and kicked the ball with him. It was an over-the-top weekend, easily the greatest time of our lives. We had been like so many families with loved ones with epilepsy. We suffered in silence. That weekend motivated us to break from our silence. To follow Coach Kill's example of speaking up for those with seizures."

—Wayne Drash

"I met Coach Kill when I was nine years old and had cancer. I learned how to talk with him about life. He immediately connected with me and we are now close friends. Shortly after we met, he took me to the players' locker room and we ran out of the tunnel at his first game here in Minnesota holding hands. It was a day I will never forget, with the crowd cheering, the high-fiving all over the place, and Coach Kill by my side.... I have made a great friend for life, and now I have been cancer free for six years. He told me that when he is having a bad day, he thinks of me [and what I have overcome]."

—Mia Gerold, friend

"I have been lucky to find my passion working with Coach Kill and his Chasing Dreams Epilepsy Fund.... [It] has been so motivating because he puts 100 percent into making a difference for these kids with epilepsy and showing them there is nothing they cannot do."

—Meredith Gretch, special projects manager,
Coach Kill Chasing Dreams Epilepsy Fund

"I loved playing for Coach Kill and I always knew he would do anything for me or for his players. He was always there for us."

—Marquis Grey, former player

"I can honestly say that there has been no other person that has had a greater impact on my life than Jerry Kill…. [He] is a football coach but his commitment to changing people lives is his higher stage."

— Melissa Haab, former director of admissions, Emporia State University

"One of the most amazing gifts he possesses: to make you feel like you are the only one that matters. Our community feels like we are partners with Jerry's Chasing Dreams Fund."

—Deb Hadley, friend

"What can I not say about Coach Kill? He changed my life…. His investment in life is with people and his connections with them. He is not like other coach—far above the rest. 'What have you done today to get better?' Those were words he has said to me that will always be with me."

—Chandler Harnish, former quarterback, Northern Illinois University

"Coach was so much fun to be around and worked so hard. He was always there for the coaches and never gave up on a player. He found a way to believe the best in everyone."

—Maddie Hayes, University of Minnesota staff

"I have the great honor of being the head football coach at a program that was built by Coach Jerry Kill…. There are no smoke and mirrors with him. He is exactly what you see."

—Nick Hill, head coach, Southern Illinois University

"The one thing that really stands out with Coach Kill is how appreciative he is for what he has and for what he has gone through in his life."

—Rich Jantz, friend

"I grew up in one of the toughest areas of Detroit. My brother spent 20 years in prison and Coach Kill encouraged me to talk about my past and come to terms with it all…. After the [the 2015 Quick Lane Bowl] he met my brother on the field, and when the two of them hugged each other, I can honestly say it was the greatest moment of my life. [He and Rebecca] saved my life."

—Jeff Jones, former player

"Coach Kill is as loyal a person as you will ever find. He is very demanding and brings out the best in all of us."

—Eric Klein, assistant coach, University of Minnesota

"*Coach Kill has created so much awareness for epilepsy and has been so involved in the community. He has changed the way people feel and what they know about epilepsy and has done more than anything I ever could have imagined.... Coach Kill and his wife, Rebecca, are the most inspiring and motivating people I know.*"

—Vicki Kopplin, executive director, Epilepsy Foundation of Minnesota

"*We need more people like Jerry Kill in this country.*"

—Ron Lankford, former superintendent of schools, Webb City

"*I was involved in a bowling fund-raiser for the University of Minnesota Children's Hospital and met with Coach Kill to see if he would allow a few players to come with me to the hospital to meet with some of the children.... His first question to me was, 'Why aren't you asking me to come?' Coach cleared his schedule and before the day was over, he spent two hours at the hospital with me, the children, and some of his players. And for the children who were too sick to participate, he went room to room. This is Jerry Kill.*"

—Dave Lee, WCCO Radio

"*Coach Kill always talks toughness, and he is a tough guy. He battled cancer and epilepsy and taught his players to always do the right thing.... He taught me how to be a leader and, most of all, a good person.*"

—Mitch Leidner, player, University of Minnesota

"*I was on Coach Kill's staff for almost 20 years. When I left the University of Minnesota I wasn't sure if I would be coaching again. Coach Kill kept in touch with me every day, sometimes twice a day, and was instrumental in me being hired at Penn State University near my home[town].... Every success that I have had in my life has been affected by Jerry Kill and I sincerely hope that someday I can find a way to repay him.*"

—Matt Limegrover, assistant football coach, Penn State University

"*Coach Kill took care of people first and then was a football coach.*"

—Roger Lipe, SIU chaplain

"*Coach Kill is a freak of nature. I used to call him the Tasmanian Devil.... When Coach Kill retired, I was relieved because I knew it was going to be the best thing for him. He is a wonderful person who never puts himself first.*"

—Sharon Lipe, Southern Illinois University staff

"After my extensive coaching search and exhausting research, I only presented one name to the university president and it was Jerry Kill.... Coach Kill was born to coach and lead young men and he has had a tremendous impact on many."

—Joel Maturi, former athletic director, University of Minnesota

"I coached with Coach Kill and have always felt that he is one of the great people of all time.... I was once asked my opinion of Coach Kill, and if I could come up with two words that best described him. Those words are: 'the best.'"

—Carl Mauck, former SIU coach and former NFL player and coach

"Coach Kill talked about loyalty all the time and I watched him live it every day. He won over the high school coaches, his players, the students, the fans, the media, and on top of it all, he won football games. When he was forced to retire due to health reasons...I was heartbroken."

—Mike Max, WCCO-TV and WCCO Radio

"The first day that I met Coach Kill, I committed to the University of Minnesota. I wanted to be around him."

—KJ Maye, former player

"[He is] of the finest human beings I have ever known. As tough as the football business is, Coach has never forgotten about the people he works with or where he came from.... Coach Kill earned everything he has received the hard way, by going to programs that needed to be fixed from high school to small colleges to the Big Ten Conference."

—Billy Miller, assistant coach, Florida State University

"I have epilepsy and diabetes. Coach Kill...got me thinking positively.... He has been a great influence on my life."

—Maja Nord, friend

"Coach Kill is different from anyone I have ever known.... He has this incredible knack of showing up at the right time, saying the right thing and doing what has to be done.... Jerry Kill is a leader, a pusher, and is always trying to improve at everything."

—Dan O'Brien, assistant coach, University of Minnesota

"I was pretty nervous when I first met Coach Kill but now that I have gotten to know him I feel like he is my older brother. He has really helped me through my illness.... [He] loves to make others happy."

—Casey O'Brien, friend

"I played for and coached with Coach Kill. He truly cared deeply about everyone on his team."

—Trevor Olson, former player and coach

"Coach Kill and I are about the same age yet he has been like a father and brother to me. We have been family for so many years.... There is an aura about Coach Kill in the special ways he does things.... I am so fortunate to have him as my friend."

—Pat Poore, assistant coach, University of Minnesota

"I am one of a very few women trainers, and he gave me the chance at Northern Illinois. He was always a pleasure to be around, even on days when things were not going so well for him."

—Kammy Powell, assistant football trainer, University of Minnesota

"What sets him apart from other coaches is his tremendous caring.... Coach Kill takes care of his staff like they are his family, and he always has."

—Angie Reeves, friend

"He is a hard worker to a fault. No one has ever worked harder. I have been with him for over 20 years and he has always been a father figure to me; he is a part of my family. He pushes everyone to be their very best and to do things the right way."

—Rob Reeves, assistant coach, University of Minnesota

"Jerry Kill knows how to lead the charge no matter the cause. He is as trustworthy as it gets and commands respect without ever demanding it.... I had the opportunity to interview Jerry shortly after he retired from coaching at Minnesota. It was perhaps the best interview I have ever been a part of because of his honesty and frankness of his situation."

—Mike Reis,
Southern Illinois University football and basketball radio announcer

"For me, it is hard to put into words what I think of Coach Kill. I get choked up just thinking about him. He is one of a kind.... I feel like I have known him my whole life."

—Steve Richardson, player, University of Minnesota

"He is so much more than a football coach. He was a developer of young men and has great personal interest in people.... I had a brother die, and other than family, Jerry was the first person to the hospital. I have never forgotten that. Football players will run through a wall for him, and he is the type of person that will do anything for you."

—John Roderique, former player and coach, Webb City High School

"A lot of my Coffeyville players have gone to play for Coach Kill.... With people it is always 'big you and little him.' Kids will lay down their lives for him."

—Dickie Rolls, administrator, Coffeyville Community College

"Coach Kill is the most unselfish coach that I have ever been around.... His tremendous compassion and caring for others is no doubt his greatest strength."

—Mark Rosen, WCCO Television Sports Director, KFAN Radio

"Coach Kill means so much to me that it is tough to put into words.... He has a way about him that [he] can always find the best in everyone."

—Joel Sambursky, former player

"Jerry Kill is without a doubt one of the best football coaches of all time.... I applaud him for his wonderful work with epilepsy and how he has been a leader in bringing awareness to this terrible disease. There is no question that Jerry Kill is the real deal!"

—T. Denny Sanford, chairman and CEO of United National Corporation

"I was with Coach Kill for many years. Every time I had an opportunity to consider another job, I realized how difficult it would be to find someone to work for better than Coach. He took care of his assistant coaches and his players. He never did anything for himself—ever. The players and the coaches always came first for him. With Coach Kill, you always knew what you were getting. A lot of coaches take over easy jobs with winning programs and great support. Coach never had one of those jobs. When he took over the program at SIU they didn't even carry football gear, caps, shirts, or jerseys in the campus bookstore, the program was so bad."

—Jay Sawvel, assistant coach, University of Minnesota

"I owe so much to Coach Kill.... He pushed me hard as a coach and even harder to get my graduate degree. I'm the last of the Coach Kill coaching tree and do not take that lightly."

—Mike Sherels, assistant coach, University of Minnesota

"His final press conference was so revealing as to who Jerry Kill is. He never talked about what he thought people wanted to hear but spoke from his heart like he always does. He has so much to give to others and I believe that he can continue doing so as long as he truly takes care of himself first."

—Dr. Brien Smith, epileptologist

"I can't say enough about Jerry. He is a great family man and...is always trying to help others."

—Doug Smith, brother-in-law

"He is not only a great football coach but a better person who makes everyone better just by being around him."

—Mark Smith, former player and coach

"It's hard for me to put in words my feelings for Coach Kill. He [was] a father figure for me."

—Paul Spicer, former player and NFL coach

"On Coach Kill's last day at practice, he took the time to talk with a young man with epilepsy that I had brought to practice. At perhaps his worst moment Coach Kill gave the young man his very best. Coach made it the highlight of my guest's life. He has made it a mission to help others and I have the highest regard for him."

—Bob Stein, Gophers All-American and former NFL player

"I have been coaching football for 54 years and I have never met a coach like Jerry Kill on or off the field. His caring for others is unequaled.... He made us go to the attic or garage and dust off our old Gopher memories and put them on the mantle atop the fireplace. The Minnesota High School Coaches Association this year renamed our Power of Influence Award the Jerry Kill Power of Influence Award."

—Ron Stolski, Brainerd [MN] High School head coach

"I played for Coach Kill at Pittsburg State and coached with him at Webb City High School. If you have the opportunity to spend only two hours with him, you will think he is your best friend. He makes you always feel special.... I heard him speak to the team at Minnesota and it was the same speech with the same passion and commitment as the ones he gave at Webb City High School."

—Kurt Thompson, former player

"If I was in a foxhole and my life was on the line I would want Jerry Kill next to me. He is the best."

—Rick Utter, former counselor, Webb City High School

"I told him when he got to Saginaw Valley that he would never be able to do what he said he was going to do. I was wrong.... Jerry Kill is my idol for what he did for our football program while he was here, but even more so for what he did for those who knew him. He became beloved. I saw players crying in the locker room after a tough loss when in the past, no one cared enough to even feel bad when we lost a football game. His impact on everyone he comes in contact with is unbelievable."

—Tom Waske, former sports information director,
Saginaw Valley State University

"You will never find a person who worked harder or was more caring.... He has impacted so many people."

—Kent Weiser, athletic director, Emporia State

"[In] my second year, I got an intestinal disease and had to give up football. I lost a ton of weight and was very sick. Coach Kill was with me every step of the way.... He has been like a father to me. I recall the day he and Rebecca had to put their dog down—and this was the same day they drove to Rochester to see me in the hospital. They...were always there for me."

—Peter Westerhaus, player, University of Minnesota

"Coach Kill is like a part of my family. He was in our home when I got drafted to the NFL. He even helped my sister get a job. He and Rebecca are the best there is. His loyalty and caring for others is absolutely unbelievable. He supported me in everything I have ever done and has made such an incredible difference in my life. I loved playing for him and the Gophers."

—Maxx Williams, former player

"From the first time we met, he treated me like we had been lifelong friends...[and now] he and Rebecca have been close friends for over 30 years."

—Gerald Young, athletic director, Carleton College

"Jerry Kill is the best man I have ever met in my life.... [He and Rebecca] are unbelievable people."

—Jim Zebrowski, assistant coach, Hamline University